More praise for
RESCUING SOCRATES

"This is an important, and timely, book about why the western canon still matters and about how great books can change lives, especially impoverished black and brown ones."
—LINDSAY JOHNS, *Times Literary Supplement*

"Montás undertakes his defense of the great books with simplicity and humility. . . . In the face of public conversations marked by fear, anger, and hostility, Montás chooses the path of vulnerability. In that, he shows the wisdom of a person who has navigated real conflict, away from the seminar table."
—ZENA HITZ, *Commonweal Magazine*

"[Montás] weaves a compelling personal narrative together with a forceful argument that reading classic texts, even those originating in predominantly white, Eurocentric cultures, is an important opportunity for underserved students of color to transform themselves and transform the inequitable social structures within which they are embedded."
—BRIAN ROSENBERG, *Chronicle of Higher Education*

"*Rescuing Socrates* is a valuable and thoughtful book both sociologically and educationally, making a contribution to the ongoing debate over the past, present, and future of liberal-arts education."
—M. D. AESCHLIMAN, *National Review*

"Montás returns the humanities to its revolutionary home, reminding us that we are, after all, talking about such radical and subversive thinkers as Augustine, Plato, Freud, and Gandhi. He teaches us, presumably like he teaches his Core Curriculum students, what those thinkers were after—and what reading them makes possible."
—JONATHAN TRAN, *Christian Century*

"One can only hope that *Rescuing Socrates* rescues others as well."
—NAOMI SCHAEFER RILEY, *Commentary*

"*Rescuing Socrates* chronicles Montás's search for truth and meaning as a young man. He describes how the Great Books have helped him thrive and make sense of difficult challenges in his life: recovering from childhood traumas (poverty, abandonment, and immigration itself), alienation among rich kids at Columbia, loss of his evangelical Christian faith, and the dissolution of his first marriage. He's infectiously passionate about making liberal education available to all, not just wealthy Ivy Leaguers confident about their comfortable futures."
—LIZA FEATHERSTONE, *Jacobin*

"This moving book is both a cry from the heart and a battle cry. It is the most convincing case yet made for liberal education as a gift to young people and indispensable for democracy. If every president, trustee, dean, and professor (of any subject) were to read it—really *read* it—hope and purpose would be restored to our colleges and universities and to all the students they serve."
—ANDREW DELBANCO, president of the Teagle Foundation and author of *College: What It Was, Is, and Should Be*

"In *Rescuing Socrates*, Roosevelt Montás tells his story of moving as a lost, lonely twelve-year-old from the Dominican Republic to New York, then eventually finding himself by studying Aristotle, Augustine, Plato, and many others in the Core Curriculum at Columbia University. Montás takes the reader on an inspiring journey where we come to realize how the power of these texts helped a young immigrant and man of color recreate his heritage and a sense of identity in a foreign land."
—ANIKA T. PRATHER, founder of The Living Water School

"This is a powerful and deeply personal defense of Great Books and liberal education. Montás has written a rousing reminder that a Great Books education is not a frivolous indulgence or a weapon in the culture wars, but a gateway to clearer thinking, meaningful human relationships, and life's most important questions."
—MOLLY WORTHEN, University of North Carolina, Chapel Hill

"Roosevelt Montás has written an absorbing and perceptive book about how he, an immigrant from a rural town in the Dominican Republic, came to New York and was engaged and transformed by reading great books. His vibrant account is an autobiography of learning. It should be read by anyone interested in reading and big ideas."
—MITCHELL COHEN, author of *The Politics of Opera: A History from Monteverdi to Mozart*

"In this beautifully written book, Roosevelt Montás presents a compelling case for the immeasurably transformative value of a true liberal education. Through his personal story and a poetic journey of the works of four great thinkers, Montás illuminates how a liberal education is essential to engaging with the most fundamental aspects of human freedom and self-determination. *Rescuing Socrates* is a touching, insightful invitation to rethink the reigning model of education in favor of one that equips us to live examined lives."
—AMNA KHALID, Carleton College

RESCUING SOCRATES

RESCUING SOCRATES

HOW THE GREAT BOOKS CHANGED MY LIFE AND WHY THEY MATTER FOR A NEW GENERATION

ROOSEVELT MONTÁS

PRINCETON UNIVERSITY PRESS

PRINCETON & OXFORD

Copyright © 2021 by Princeton University Press

Princeton University Press is committed to the protection of copyright and the intellectual property our authors entrust to us. Copyright promotes the progress and integrity of knowledge. Thank you for supporting free speech and the global exchange of ideas by purchasing an authorized edition of this book. If you wish to reproduce or distribute any part of it in any form, please obtain permission.

Requests for permission to reproduce material from this work should be sent to permissions@press.princeton.edu

Published by Princeton University Press
41 William Street, Princeton, New Jersey 08540
99 Banbury Road, Oxford OX2 6JX

press.princeton.edu

All Rights Reserved

First paperback printing, 2023
Paper ISBN 978-0-691-224398
Cloth ISBN 978-0-691-200392
ISBN (e-book) 978-0-691-224381

British Library Cataloging-in-Publication Data is available

Editorial: Peter Dougherty and Alena Chekanov
Production Editorial: Brigitte Pelner
Jacket/Cover Design: Karl Spurzem
Production: Erin Suydam
Publicity: Alyssa Sanford (US) and Carmen Jimenez (UK)
Copyeditor: Patricia Fogarty

Jacket/Cover Images: (1) Life Preserver—Shutterstock, (2) Statue of Socrates at the Academy of Athens, built by Leonidas Drossis (d. 1880)

This book has been composed in Arno and Brandon Grotesque

Printed in the United States of America

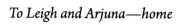

To Leigh and Arjuna—home

CONTENTS

INTRODUCTION

The Case

This book is about my liberal education. It is also about the practice of liberal education in today's university. It is both a personal and a polemical book. Because my thinking about education is inseparable from my particular experience, this book is a meditation on how liberal education has shaped my own life. My arguments and observations draw on my career as a college professor and academic administrator, but the driving force behind this book is the way in which liberal education has altered and enriched the trajectory of my life.

That trajectory began in 1973 in Cambita Garabitos, a rural town in the Dominican Republic that was still immersed in the agrarian and pre-industrial rhythms of the nineteenth century. On May 26, 1985, I left Cambita for New York. The flight was only three and half hours long, but the distance I traveled on that day was in many ways incalculable. And it was again a long distance from learning English as a second language in the over-crowded classrooms of IS 61 in Corona, Queens, to enrolling as a freshman at Columbia University in 1991. I eventually earned a PhD from Columbia and have been teaching humanities there for twenty years. My liberal education has given me a way of making sense of this complicated trajectory.

The idea of liberal education goes back to the ancient democracy of Athens, where it was conceived as the education

appropriate for free citizens. Aristotle described it as an education "given not because it is useful or necessary but because it
is noble and suitable for a free person."[1] All Athenian citizens,
the sort of "free persons" Aristotle had in mind, participated in
government by voting directly on the adoption of laws, holding
political office, deliberating on juries, and serving in the army.
The point of liberal education was to prepare citizens for these
civic responsibilities. To this day, democracies depend on a
citizenry capable of discharging the duties for which a liberal
education prepared Athenian citizens. Indeed, the possibility
of democracy hinges on the success or failure of liberal
education.

But the term "liberal education," like its cousin "the liberal
arts," is not well understood even among academics. Outside
academia, it gets a cold reception, combining the political bag-
gage of the word "liberal" with the reputed uselessness of studying art. One recent critic warned that "putting the words *liberal*
and *arts* together is a branding disaster."[2] Common substitutes,
in part because of their innocuousness, include "general education," "core competencies," "transferable skills," or even simply
"the humanities." But these alternatives fail to convey the central feature of a liberal education: its concern with the condition
of human freedom and self-determination.

In the slave democracy of Athens, liberal education was distinguished from the education of an enslaved person or of a
"vulgar craftsman." Today, it is distinguished from professional,

---

1. Aristotle, *Politics*, C.D.C. Reeve, trans. (Indianapolis and Cambridge: Hackett
Publishing Company, 1998), VIII, 1338a, 30–31, p. 230.

2. Brandon Busteed, "Higher Education: Drop the Term 'Liberal Arts,'" Gallup
News, Opinion (Aug. 16, 2017), https://news.gallup.com/opinion/gallup/216275
/higher-education-drop-term-liberal-arts.aspx?g_source=Opinion&g_medium
=lead&g_campaign=tiles.

technical, or vocational education. Liberal education looks to the meaning of a human life beyond the requirements of subsistence—instead of asking how to make a living, liberal education asks what living is for. "These studies," says Aristotle, "are undertaken for their own sake, whereas those relating to work are necessary and for the sake of things other than themselves."[3] Liberal education concerns the human yearning to go beyond questions of survival to questions of existence.

In American colleges and universities, liberal education is typically offered as required courses, often in the humanities and social sciences, that lie outside of the student's major. With some exceptions, especially in recent years,[4] colleges and universities elsewhere in the world don't offer this general foundation for higher learning but focus directly on specialized studies.[5]

o o o

My liberal education began with my father's Marxist-inspired opposition to the Dominican strongman Joaquín Balaguer in the 1970s, and the political tradition through which he justified his activism. Some of his political activity took place in the open— debates and public denunciations, strikes and demonstrations,

---

3. *Politics*, 1338a, 10–12.

4. For a useful survey of recent efforts in Europe, see Marijk van der Wende, "The Emergence of the Liberal Arts and Sciences Education in Europe: A Comparative Perspective," in *Higher Education Policy* 24:2 (June 2011), pp. 233–253.

5. For a provocative treatment of the peculiarly American tradition of liberal arts education, see Jose María Torralba, "Educación Liberal *Made in the USA*: De cómo se inventaron las humanidades," in *Falsos saberes: La suplantación del conocimiento en la cultura contemporánea,* Juan Arana, ed. (Madrid: Editorial Biblioteca Nueva, 2013), pp. 61–74.

fundraising and organizing. Some of it was clandestine—secret meetings, training in guerrilla tactics, sheltering individuals sought by the authorities, establishing relations with militant leftists throughout Latin America. Although he had only a sixth-grade education, his politics were steeped in an intellectual tradition of which he was only vaguely aware, but which I began to internalize along with my first intimations of who I was in the world.

But my formal liberal education began when I entered Columbia University as a freshman and came across its celebrated Core Curriculum. Sometimes described as a Great Books program, the Core Curriculum is a set of courses in literary and philosophical classics—as well as art, music, and science—in which all students study and discuss a prescribed list of works that begins in antiquity and moves chronologically to the present. The Core, as it is commonly known, constitutes the distinctive backbone of the education offered by Columbia College, Columbia University's residential liberal arts college. Legendary for its rigor, the Core is a kind of intellectual baptism that goes back more than a century and harkens to a time when an introduction to the Western tradition of learning was recognized as a self-evident good.

Today, Columbia's Core Curriculum stands as a kind of relic, with no other major university requiring a common course of study in what used to be called "the classics." Many schools do continue to offer liberal education through the common study of important books, but usually on an elective basis.[6] After

---

6. Among big research universities, the Core model survives in programs like Yale's Directed Studies, Stanford's Structured Liberal Education program, and the University of Chicago's Core Curriculum. St. John's College, in Annapolis and Santa Fe, has carried the logic of the Core to its maximum application, organizing its entire undergraduate program around the common reading and discussion of original texts.

earning a PhD in English, my first faculty job was as a Lecturer in the Columbia Core Curriculum, and I then served as its chief administrator from 2008 to 2018.

I had come to the United States from a mountain town in the Dominican Republic a few days before my twelfth birthday, not speaking English, and never before having been even close to an airplane. I came with my older brother, who was seventeen. My mother had arrived in the United States two years earlier. Immediately after finding a minimum-wage job in a garment factory, she made arrangements for my brother and me to join her. That had been the whole point of accepting life as a nobody in Nueba Yol, which is what we called all of the United States. We would live in a place called Queens.

The city that greeted us was the menacing New York of the 1980s, and like many other Dominican immigrants, we arrived poor, disoriented, and with little notion of what would happen next. Along with the greenness and wonder of a country boy, I landed at JFK International Airport with a head full of lice and a belly full of tropical parasites. In many respects, I was an unlikely candidate for the Ivy League.

After two years of bilingual education in the local public school and four years at the local public high school, I found myself beginning an unimaginably strange life as a freshman at Columbia College. There I began to make sense of the world and of my place in it through the social and intellectual initiation that is the Core Curriculum.

○ ○ ○

Many schools and programs committed to a Core text approach to liberal education gather together annually under the auspices of the Association for Core Texts and Courses (https://www.coretexts.org).

Liberal education has always been a hard sell. People fortunate enough to have had it often describe it as a life-altering experience. But those who haven't had it don't usually feel that their lives are less rich or less fulfilling for lacking it. With higher education increasingly seen in transactional terms—with students paying exorbitant amounts of money to gain a leg up in a fiercely competitive job environment—it is easy to see how liberal education might be regarded as a waste of time. Politicians, the general public, and even university leaders often dismiss it as impractical and pointless—an antiquated affectation of privilege. But liberal education has always had formidable defenders. From Plato and Aristotle, to Cicero and Marcus Aurelius, to Erasmus and Galileo, to Virginia Woolf and W.E.B. Du Bois, to contemporary torchbearers like Andrew Delbanco, Martha Nussbaum, and Fareed Zakaria, eminent thinkers have insisted on the value and indispensability of liberal education.

But the case is persistently hard to make. Part of the difficulty stems from the nature of the good that a liberal education delivers. Communicating its value typically demands an artificial compression, a pointing to a bottom line that, like the plot summary of a great novel, can never convey the experience of reading the novel itself. In both cases, the value of the thing cannot be extracted and delivered apart from the experience of the thing. So arguments about the importance of liberal education always and necessarily fall short, and are typically most appreciated by those who least need it.

This book is a meditation on and an introduction to the experience of liberal education. Rather than offer a battery of arguments, I try to bring the reader closer to the experience of liberal education through encounters with some of the human questions that lie at its heart. I do this through discussions of four authors that have deeply influenced the way I think about these questions: Saint Augustine, Plato, Sigmund Freud, and Mahatma Gandhi. My four companions come from worlds that are in many ways alien to our own, but they all speak with intimate familiarity about human experiences that we all share. This book is in part an invitation to that conversation.

Augustine, Plato, Freud, and Gandhi. Two ancients and two moderns. One African, two Europeans, and one Indian. A Christian saint, a pagan philosopher, a Jewish atheist, and a Hindu ascetic. A teacher of rhetoric who converted to Christianity and became its most influential theologian, an aristocrat whose young heart was conquered by philosophy and who went on to lay the foundations for Western learning, a researcher in neurophysiology who abandoned the lab and invented a new way of understanding the mind, and a timid Indian lawyer who became a Mahatma, a "Great Soul," and guided a nation to independence.

Each of these writers is, in his own way, a canonical figure who commands the attention of any serious student of the contemporary world. The Columbia Core Curriculum consists almost exclusively of such figures. Authors like Homer, Dante, Shakespeare, and Woolf are semi-permanent fixtures, while others like Sappho, Ovid, and Milton cycle in and out of the required reading list according to the shifting consensus of the faculty. But I write about Augustine, Plato, Freud, and Gandhi not because of their canonical status but because of the role they have played in my development as an individual and as a teacher. In one way or another, each of them experienced an inner transformation that made them into the figures we know today. In each case, the motive force was the relentless pursuit of self-understanding—the very kind of understanding that liberal education takes as its ultimate goal. This book is a reflection on how they have figured into my own search for self-understanding and into my work as a liberal arts teacher and administrator.

In each of the four chapters that follow, I weave together three strands: a discussion of the work of each author, a meditation on how each has helped me make sense of my own life, and a critique of the practice of liberal education in the contemporary university. With the first strand, I try to make the texts accessible to a general audience. With the second, I reflect on how they can illuminate a person's lived experience. With the third, I show how liberal education is impaired and imperiled in higher education and argue for its revitalization. These various threads mix and flow into each other guided not by a grand argumentative design, but by the idiosyncrasies of how my particular life has unfolded.

o o o

I first read Saint Augustine's spiritual autobiography, *Confessions*, as a freshman at Columbia. Among the fundamental renegotiations of identity I was undergoing that first year of college was a reassessment of the fervent Pentecostal Christianity I had embraced shortly after coming to the US. It was beginning to dawn on me that my conversion had been midwifed by loneliness, dislocation, and a desperate need for belonging.

Augustine's journey to Christianity was shaped by books. It was through his various encounters with texts that, as he says, "Lord, you turned my attention back to myself."[7] In the *Confessions*, he again and again reflects on people being inwardly and irrevocably transformed through the act of reading. He himself

___

7. Saint Augustine, *Confessions*, Henry Chadwick, trans. (Oxford: Oxford University Press, 2008), p. 144.

was inwardly and irrevocably transformed through reading. In the winter of 1992, I was reading the *Confessions* and trying to find in that book, as in everything else in those days, a way to salvation. I, too, was being irrevocably transformed—in ways that were immediately evident to me and in ways that I am still trying to understand.

Though a work of considerable philosophical importance and theological complexity, what emerges most vividly in the *Confessions* is the portrait of an individual who was tenderly sensitive to the existential pain of the human condition. He disarms the reader with his impish curiosity and the kind of irreverent honesty that can ask God to "grant me chastity and continence, but not yet."[8] No writer from antiquity comes across to us as so fully human, so psychologically intricate and convincing, so like ourselves, as Augustine.

Perhaps *Confessions* was particularly compelling to me because in it I found a language for inner exploration. The urgency of Augustine's search for an intellectually and psychologically satisfying account of his own being resonated profoundly with my urgency to understand the life I was living and the world in which I found myself.

I encountered Saint Augustine's *Confessions* in Columbia's famous first-year requirement Literature Humanities. "Lit Hum" was first offered in 1937 with the aim of introducing an increasingly "philistine" student body to Masterpieces of European Literature and Philosophy, as the official name of the class unself-consciously declares. With this year-long tour of literary "masterpieces," I was introduced to a conversation that stretched deep into antiquity. Each week, I would encounter some strange and ancient writer who would provoke me with

---

8. *Confessions*, p. 145.

serious and unsettling questions, and who would feel at once remote and familiar. In this course, I was also thrust into a conversation with the entire first-year class at Columbia, who were, like me, required to sit around a table for four hours each week and talk to each other about the books we were reading. While neither the minds I was touching through the books nor the minds and bodies I was touching through the class were entirely decipherable to me, the triangulation that this arrangement made possible became, over weeks and months, my way of centering and locating myself.

Literature Humanities was invented by John Erskine, who first offered it at Columbia as an honors course simply called General Honors; it proposed the radical idea—radical even in the 1930s—of "reading, in translation, one classic each week." Today, the idea is not only radical but also impossible to execute in most universities. Columbia has bucked the intellectual and academic trend in maintaining the course, along with a handful of others similarly conceived, at the center of its undergraduate curriculum.

o o o

In my sophomore year of high school, I came upon a remarkable book in a garbage pile next to the house where we rented an apartment in Queens. It was the second volume of the pretentiously bound Harvard Classics series, and it contained a set of dialogues by Plato that record the last days of Socrates's life. This first encounter with Socrates was as fortuitous as it was decisive. There is probably no better introduction to the life of the mind than Socrates's defense of his philosophic activity in these dialogues.

For over a decade, I have used these same dialogues every summer to introduce low-income high school students to a world that, almost without exception, had been until then inaccessible and inconceivable to them. The series of short dialogues are set in the days leading up to Socrates's execution. He emerges in them vividly and heroically. Throughout his ordeal, he insists that "the good life, the beautiful life, and the just life are the same,"[9] and that no matter what the city of Athens might threaten to do to him, he cannot give up the practice of philosophy. The youth of Athens love him, but the authorities find him an unbearable nuisance and, as Jesus would come to seem to the Romans, a dangerous political liability.

Indeed, the citizens of Athens, finding seventy-year-old Socrates guilty of corrupting the youth and introducing new gods into the city, condemn him to death. Socrates accepts the verdict, rejects the plan his friends hatch to whisk him away from prison before the execution, and in obedience to the laws of the city he held dear, drinks the poison at the appointed hour, surrounded by the very friends he was accused of corrupting, and philosophizing to the very end.

Every year, I witness Socrates bringing students—my high school students as well as my Columbia students—to serious contemplation of the ultimately existential issues his philosophy demands we grapple with. My students from low-income households do not take this sort of thinking to be the exclusive privilege of a social elite. In fact, they find in it a vision of dignity and excellence that is not constrained by material limitations. Some of these students, as was the case with me, will go on to elite colleges and find themselves surrounded by peers far wealthier and far better educated than they. Socrates whispers

---

9. *Crito*, 48b, p. 48, in Plato, *The Trial and Death of Socrates*, trans. by G.M.A Grube, rev. by John M. Cooper, 3rd ed. (Indianapolis and Cambridge: Hackett Publishing Company, 2000).

to them not to mistake these marks of privilege for true expressions of merit and to find in their own intellectual integrity a source of self-worth and self-respect that surpasses any material advantage their peers might have over them.

When making the case for liberal education to low-income students and families, I often point out that there is a long tradition of steering working-class students toward an education in servitude, an education in obedience and docility, an education in not asking questions. The idea that liberal education is only for the already privileged, for the pampered elite, is a way of carrying on this odious tradition. It is a way of putting liberal education out of the reach of the people who would most benefit from it—precisely the people who have historically been denied the tools of political agency. I ask them to take a look at who sends their children to liberal arts colleges and at what liberal arts college graduates go on to do with their "useless" education. Far from a pointless indulgence for the elite, liberal education is, in fact, the most powerful tool we have to subvert the hierarchies of social privilege that keep those who are down, down.

o o o

The aura of frivolous self-indulgence that surrounds liberal education also attaches to Freudian psychoanalysis and its contemporary offspring, psychotherapy. The similarity is not accidental. Both practices demand a certain distance from the pressing business of everyday life. But the parallels don't stop there. The psychotherapeutic hour and the liberal arts seminar both bring into focus the deepest questions that concern us as human beings. In both cases, participants—therapists and patients on the one hand, and teachers and students on the other—engage in a kind of inquiry that, when successful, produces insights with the power to transform one's entire life.

Sigmund Freud was among the first thinkers I encountered at Columbia—in a summer program for incoming students who, like me, were economically and academically "disadvantaged." Though I did not read Freud himself that summer, the professor who taught the class made frequent references to his ideas. That first introduction was enough to drive home Freud's central insight: the pervasiveness of unconscious mental processes in what we think, what we do, and who we take ourselves to be. Freud alerted me to the fact that my own mind was not the transparent self I had always taken it to be, but rather a kind of *terra incognita,* a place full of mysteries and shadowy arrangements that, despite their invisibility, conditioned my personality. As that perception matured and deepened, my own mind became the overriding subject of study in and outside of the classroom.

Like a schismatic religion, Freud's legacy has splintered into many sects, and it has been vigorously disputed, reinterpreted, expanded, and sometimes discredited. But his signature approach to the investigation of the mind, most commonly known today as "talk therapy," continues to thrive, even among Freud's detractors. A few practitioners carry on Freud's classic modality: psychoanalysis—an intensive form of talk therapy that requires four or five sessions a week. In psychoanalysis, many of Freud's key concepts—the unconscious, the significance of dreams, transference, infantile sexuality, etc.—are taken seriously as guideposts for self-exploration.

By the time I read Freud in the Core curriculum as a sophomore, I had become accustomed to the fact that nearly everyone I had met at Columbia was either in therapy or had been in therapy. In time, I myself underwent a six-year psychoanalysis that spanned most of my time in graduate school and through which I began to unwind some of the psychic tangles my life had accumulated.

In his work, which was as much philosophical and literary as it was clinical, Freud set out to uncover the underlying mechanisms that govern the functioning of the human mind. As a clinician, he is largely dismissed, with, one has to admit, some good reasons. But his significance as a thinker who complicated our notions of personal agency, consciousness, sexuality, and self-understanding remains formidable. His ideas have implications for how one understands one's own life, but also for how one reads a book, how one looks at a painting, and how one hears the words of others. His efforts left us a set of oddly shaped but effective tools for the task of self-exploration.

o o o

I started teaching Mohandas Gandhi in my section of Introduction to Contemporary Civilization in the West a few years before it was incorporated into the required reading list for all sophomores. I did so using the small amount of discretion each instructor has to introduce material that supplements the common syllabus. Eventually, Gandhi was added to the common reading list and has remained there since 2012.

I started reading Gandhi with my students in part because I wanted them to grapple with a thinker who, while deeply influenced by the "Western" tradition we had spent a year studying, was rooted in a different, ancient, at times alien way of understanding the world. Gandhi challenges notions that are taken for granted in the European political tradition—notions like the paramount value of a human life, the legitimacy of violence when used in self-defense, the primacy of individual rights, and the desirability of technological mastery over nature. In his writing, political activity, and manner of living, Gandhi cast a harsh and startling light on some of the premises underlying what we call Western civilization.

Gandhi understood the civilization that emerged from the Industrial Revolution as a materialist worldview that placed wealth, comfort, and longevity as the highest human goods. For him, the inescapable consequence of this value system was the violence, rapacity, and disregard for human and non-human life that he saw in European colonial endeavors around the world. As an antidote, Gandhi proposed an approach to individual and collective flourishing focused on the inner capacity for *swaraj*— that is, for self-rule, independence or, to use the banner word of the Western political enlightenment, freedom. In my experience, students find their encounter with Gandhi to be personally and politically eye-opening.

Unlike the other writers I discuss in this book, I only came to Gandhi after completing my formal education. Ever since college, I had been curious about his *Autobiography*, which a friend who was an avowed atheist told me had nearly brought her to believe in God. I finally got around to reading Gandhi's *Autobiography* not long after graduate school. A year earlier, I had adopted a daily practice of meditation and was trying to understand the way in which this habit was slowly transforming my mind. Gandhi's rootedness in the same matrix of spiritual practices that brought meditation to the West heightened my interest. By then, I had also spent several years teaching major Western texts in Columbia's Core Curriculum. I wanted to branch out of this tradition and get a taste of what else there was. Gandhi was a perfect way to start this. He had meaning for me as an intellectual project and also as a model for probing and experimenting with some of the deepest forces in my psyche.

Gandhi subtitled his autobiography *The Story of My Experiments with Truth*. Perhaps more than anything else, Gandhi saw himself as a researcher investigating the nature of human existence. The governing passion of his life was his quest for "Truth." More than once, he brought himself to the verge of death in the course of his "experiments." "What I have been trying and pining to achieve these thirty years," he wrote in the *Autobiography* "is self-realization, to see God face to face, to attain *Moksha* [ultimate liberation from the cycle of death and rebirth]. I live and move and have my being in pursuit of this goal. All that I do by way of speaking and writing, and all of my ventures in the political field are directed to this same end."[10]

Gandhi's primary field of experimentation was himself. His experiments involved his physical self through diet, celibacy, and renunciations of every sort, as well as his spiritual self through prayer, meditation, and devotional study. But if his own person was the arena of experimentation, his laboratory was the broad society in which he lived. In working out the tensions between his quest for personal liberation and the societal commitments it required, Gandhi developed a way of merging radical spirituality with the worldly turmoil of national politics.

It was Gandhi's unique fusion of religion and politics that led me to start teaching him in Introduction to Contemporary Civilization. Reflecting on this relationship as he closed the *Autobiography*, he noted that "those who say that religion has nothing to do with politics do not know what religion means."[11] For Gandhi, the personal was political, but not in the

---

10. Mohandas K. Gandhi, *Autobiography: The Story of My Experiments with Truth*, Mahadev Desai, trans. (New York: Dover Publications), 1983, p. viii.

11. *Autobiography*, p. 454.

way that contemporary activists conceive of that link. Writing to his nephew, he advised him to "not carry unnecessarily on your head the burden of emancipating India. Apply everything to yourself. Nobility of soul consists in realizing that you are yourself India. In your emancipation is the emancipation of India."[12]

Gandhi's idea of religion boiled down to two basic principles: truth and non-violence. These were the same principles behind satyagraha—the mass movement of non-violent resistance that forced both South African and Indian authorities to release their iron grip on the lives of ordinary Indians.

For many students, as was the case for me, Gandhi comes as a revelation. Appearing toward the end of the Contemporary Civilization course, a year in which many students find their most basic assumptions about who they are and what the world is challenged and de-stabilized, Gandhi offers a view of a morally coherent universe, where concepts like truth, love, self-sacrifice, and even salvation can still hold meaning.

Gandhi's practical and seemingly non-theoretical conception of truth and non-violence also offers a powerful counterpoint to the postmodern current in Western learning. This current emerged in the late nineteenth century with Friedrich Nietzsche and has become a dominant framework in the social sciences and the academic humanities. Its fundamental challenge to the notions of truth, virtue, and reason strike at the heart of liberal education and help explain the inhospitable intellectual climate in which liberal education finds itself in the university. Today, the defense of liberal education demands a response to this

---

12. Mohandas K. Gandhi, *The Collected Works of Mahatma Gandhi* (henceforth *CWMG*) (New Delhi: Government of India, Ministry of Information and Broadcasting, 1956–1984), 100 vols., Vol. 10, pp. 206–207.

postmodern challenge. Gandhi's life and work provide the grounds for such a response.

o o o

I was admitted to Columbia University through its Opportunity Programs—an admissions category created to meet the requirements of the New York State Higher Education Opportunity Program (HEOP), which provides generous financial and academic support to low-income students. It had been six years since I had arrived from the Dominican Republic. Everyone in the know at Columbia understood that a HEOP student belonged to a cohort of poor, mainly black and brown students with SAT scores below the mean of other admitted students. We stuck out on campus to veteran faculty, experienced administrators, savvy students, and each other. Waiting for me and my group of about twenty HEOP students was Literature Humanities, that mammoth and daring course that has greeted every new Columbia student since 1937.

I was still learning a lot of new English vocabulary that first year of college and laboriously piecing together things that were common knowledge to just about everyone around me. Lit Hum was my first full immersion into American culture, or at least the particular slice of American culture that was the Columbia College entering class of 1991. So my freshman year was an education not only in the works of the Lit Hum syllabus, but in that which for everyone else went without saying—the givens of the social world in which I was beginning to live. And those two forms of education mingled together, illuminating each other, and etching particularity on each other. That mingling happened in conversations in the classroom and in the Dean's Office of the School of General Studies, where I secured a twenty-hour-a-week work-study job. I did not contribute much to the conversations in the classroom; I did not feel familiar enough to allow myself public opinions. I mainly observed my peers. I was studying them as well as the books. Two hours on Monday and two hours on Wednesday. Weekends spent sitting in my room and in the lounges of my dorm, reading.

By the end of that first year, my education included a bank of information about how people behaved around those old books and the big questions they raised: a first and tentative sense of the norms of expression, affect, and sensibility of the peculiar world where I had landed. I was observing and absorbing styles of expression, accents, quirks, tones, turns of phrases, ways of being a person. Yet the insights of that first year were more often about myself than about the books I was reading or the peers I was watching. I didn't know then that this is precisely where the greatest value of a liberal education lies: in turning students' eyes inward, into an exploration of their own humanity under the provocation of works that have proven their power to inspire just such self-reflection.

I had come into Lit Hum expecting to learn about texts and authors, and little suspecting that these concrete aspects of what I'd learn would prove to be mere vehicles for a far deeper and transformative kind of education. That inward education came slowly, almost unconsciously. It was not like the flipping of a switch, but like the dawning of a day. Many of the conversations we had in the classroom about the books and ideas that were rushing upon us went over my head, but like a recurring tide that leaves behind a thin layer of sediment each time it comes, eventually forming recognizable structures, the intensive reading and twice-weekly discussions were coalescing into an altogether new sense of who I was and of the possibilities of my life.

My Lit Hum professor was an old veteran by the time I showed up in his classroom with unkempt hair and clothes that adhered to no known style. He passed away while I was in graduate school. He was one of those figures one almost never finds in research universities any more: an undergraduate teacher with tenure. When Columbia College and the University's graduate programs merged their faculties in the late 1980s, Wallace Gray continued to teach undergraduates only, becoming the longest-serving Literature Humanities instructor on the faculty. I remember him saying to my class that he hoped to die with a piece of chalk in his hand, which he very nearly did. I remember him shedding tears while reading to the class from Dostoevsky's *The Brothers Karamazov.* I remember his attentiveness to me.

He liked to write plays, but not scholarly books. His one book, *Homer to Joyce,* is a collection of eighteen sparkling essays on the books in the Lit Hum syllabus. On the last day of class, he inscribed my copy of the book. I didn't take full note of what he had written there until many years later, when I was placing his book on my shelves in the new office I was to occupy as Director of the Center for the Core Curriculum. The printed dedication of the book reads, in capital letters, "FOR MY STUDENTS"; underneath that, dated May 1, 1992, he wrote: "And especially for Roosevelt Montás—we need young men of your intelligence and sensitivity to carry on the humanist tradition in teaching." I am still humbled that Wallace Gray would say that of me. When he wrote it, he could not know that he would die of a heart attack nine years later, at age seventy-four, and I could not know that what he was writing on my book was a prophecy.

CHAPTER 1

Turning My Attention Back to Myself: Saint Augustine

I was not the only Columbia student reading Saint Augustine's *Confessions* in January 1992. In fact, the entire first-year class was reading it that same week as part of the required year-long course in Western literary classics, Literature Humanities. The twenty-two students that made up my section of "Lit Hum" would come together for two hours on Mondays and Wednesdays to talk about this and other "great books." Our teacher was Wallace Gray, a legendary English professor who was already an old man by the time I took his section of Lit Hum.

I signed up for Professor Gray's section because I had overheard someone in front of me in the registration line saying that his brother had gone to Columbia and taken Lit Hum with Gray, "and he told me it changed his life." This was a nice bit of what sociologists call "social capital" that I just happened to snatch from an August breeze in front of Pulitzer Hall. The College's admissions literature had claimed that I'd learn a lot from just being around my fellow students. Maybe this was part of what they meant. So I filled out the appropriate circles in the "bubble sheet" with a number 2 pencil and started reading in earnest the first six books of the *Iliad*, which had been assigned for the first class.

> Sing, goddess, the anger of Peleus' son Achilleus
> and its devastation, which put pains thousandfold upon
>   the Achaians,
> hurled in their multitudes to the house of Hades strong
>   souls
> of heroes, but gave their bodies to be the delicate feasting
> of dogs, of all birds, and the will of Zeus was
>   accomplished
> since that time when first there stood in division of
>   conflict
> Atreus' son the lord of men and brilliant Achilleus.[1]

So began my Columbia education, as has that of the tens of thousands of Columbia freshmen (and, as of 1983, freshwomen) who have taken Literature Humanities. The course was introduced as a first-year requirement in the fall of 1937, taught by an interdisciplinary faculty of mixed rank that included Jacques Barzun, Mark Van Doren, and Lionel Trilling. The *Iliad* was then, and has continued to be, the first book on the syllabus. Like probably most other high school seniors headed for Columbia, I had secured a copy of the *Iliad* soon after my admission. Actually, I got a copy even before admission as a Christmas present from my high school social studies teacher, John Philippides. Mr. Philippides had encouraged me to apply to Columbia, and—I realize in retrospect—was doing his best to prepare me for it. Trying to make sense of this monster of a text is an

---

1. Homer, *Iliad*, Richmond Lattimore, trans. (Chicago: University of Chicago Press, 1961), p. 59.

intellectual initiation that all Columbia students undergo, a kind of rite of passage.

Even though I had read these lines half a dozen times already, they still seemed thoroughly strange on that sultry afternoon—dissonant, stilted, and jagged in a way I found difficult to parse. Goddess. Hades. Heroes. Souls. Bodies. Dogs. How do you sing anger? How do you sing devastation? Does it mean more than singing *about* anger, *about* devastation? It must. Does the poet mean "Goddess, sing *through* me"? Or does he mean "Sing, goddess, and I will listen"? What sense can I make, and how, of a voice from maybe 3,000 years ago in a language that no longer exists? What value could there be in my reading this and thinking about it seriously? And talking about it? What insights would my professor, who was surely a very distinguished and learned person, transmit about this bizarre poem?

These questions, and more, proliferating and cascading without stop with each page I read, would soon begin to find answers, or at least find a place in my growing awareness of the dimensions of my ignorance. And each book on the syllabus—the *Odyssey*, the Hymn to Demeter, the *Oresteia* trilogy, Sophocles's Theban plays, Euripides's *Bacchae*, Aristophanes's *Clouds*, Herodotus's and Thucydides's histories—all in the first few weeks of my new life living in a dorm and being a Columbia student—each of these books would bring its own bewilderments, provocations, and recognitions.

o o o

Literature Humanities was modeled on a course invented by John Erskine in 1919 at Columbia College called General Honors. The course was based on the simple but radical idea that undergraduates would benefit from an intensive, non-disciplinary course consisting of reading, usually in translation, one classic each week in literature, philosophy, and history. "Why not treat the *Iliad* and the *Odyssey* and other masterpieces," asked Erskine, "as though they were recent publications, calling for immediate investigation and discussion?"[2] Anyone not familiar with the inner workings of academia might wonder that this isn't already a standard part of a college education and would probably never suspect the difficulty and, in most cases, the impossibility of offering such a course.

To begin with, as Erskine discovered, "It immediately became clear that the faculty could not define a great book; at least they couldn't agree on a definition" (168). This impasse nearly scuttled the whole plan. To this day, though animated by different concerns, reaching consensus on what matters most continues to be a fundamental impediment to the adoption of common curricula in undergraduate general education. Columbia College's Committee on Instruction, "worn out by futile talk," left that task of selecting the course's "great books" to Erskine himself. Erskine drew up a list of about seventy-five books, guided by the remarkably ecumenical principle that "a great book is one that has meaning and continues to have meaning, for a variety of people over a long period of time" (168–169).

Erskine's General Honors was offered to juniors and seniors in small groups from 1920 to 1928, when he left to become President of the new Julliard School of Music. After a brief hiatus, the course was resurrected in 1932, by Jacques Barzun and others, with the innocent name of Colloquium on Important

---

2. John Erskine, *My Life as a Teacher* (Philadelphia and New York: J. B. Lippincott Company, 1948), p. 166.

Books.[3] The new name self-consciously avoided the term "great books" to signal its distance from the "Great Books heresy"—the notion that a specific set of "Great Books" constitutes the authoritative foundation of "Western culture."[4] The Colloquium, as would become evident in the next several years, also aspired to be more democratic than General Honors, which was restricted to a few highly qualified students.

The General Honors course met on Wednesday nights in multiple sections of twenty-five to thirty students, each led by "two instructors selected for their disposition to disagree with each other" (170). One famous and consequential section of General Honors was taught by Mark Van Doren and Mortimer Adler. Adler would introduce the Great Books idea to the then Dean of the Yale Law School, Robert Maynard Hutchins, who was rumored at the time never to have read a single novel.[5] Hutchins got hooked and, upon becoming president of the University of Chicago in 1929, brought Adler along to install a Great Books program at the center of the undergraduate curriculum. The Great Books Movement had been born.[6]

In 1937, Columbia took the daring step of turning the Colloquium on Important Books, which stood at the pinnacle of the undergraduate curriculum and admitted only the College's most serious and ambitious students, into a universal first-year

---

3. See Alan Willard Brown, "The Columbia College Colloquium on Important Books," *Journal of General Education* 2:4 (1948), pp. 278–286, JSTOR, www.jstor.org /stable/27795222, accessed 29 Dec. 2020.

4. Transcript of unpublished talk.

5. Jacques Barzun, "The Birth of the Humanities Course," *Columbia College Today* (Fall 1987), p. 15.

6. Alex Beam's *A Great Idea at the Time: The Rise, Fall, and Curious Afterlife of the Great Books* (New York: PublicAffairs, 2008) offers an engaging and lighthearted account of the movement and its aftermath.

requirement. Reflecting on the early years of Lit Hum on the occasion of its fiftieth anniversary, Quentin Anderson, another distinguished teacher and literary scholar, who began teaching the course in the fall of 1940 and chaired the program from 1956 to 1961, recalled some of the questions the experiment raised:

> What had Columbia College undertaken to do!? Did they somehow think we could replace the education of English gentlemen by reading a score of books in translation? Reading them, moreover, in a hurry and drawing on a staff that had itself been trained in particular disciplines and could claim no more than amateur status in relation to most of the reading list. Was the course more than a pretense of stanching a cultural wound that could never conceivably be healed? Moreover, was not the very act of choosing the very books to be read in the given year an implied aggression? Did we think ourselves capable of defining what was essential to the Western tradition?[7]

I did not arrive at Columbia with any desire to be an English gentleman, or even any notion of what that was. But I did go to Columbia with a gaping lack of exposure to the culture of higher education. Besides a fervent immersion in Biblical exegesis, and what I had picked up as a child from my father's self-education in Marxism, I was as ignorant of letters as probably any student in Columbia's near 250-year history had ever been.

Erskine had formulated his initial proposal for General Honors in 1917 in response to the complaints of older faculty colleagues about "the literary ignorance of the younger generation."[8] That same year, Columbia College had dropped

---

7. Transcript of unpublished talk.
8. *My Life as a Teacher*, p. 165.

its Latin language entrance requirement, which meant that its student body would increasingly come from the public schools of New York, with its many immigrants, and less from the elite college preparatory schools, with their emphasis on classical languages.[9]

"One of the commonest references that one hears with regard to Columbia," noted Frederic Keppel, the College Dean who oversaw this transition, "is that its position at the gateway of European immigration makes it socially uninviting to students who come from homes of refinement." As Keppel acknowledged explicitly, the problem was the number of Jewish students on campus, or rather the "slowly dying prejudice" behind the ubiquitous question "Isn't Columbia overrun with European Jews?" Keppel defended Columbia's admission of some Jewish students, noting that those "who have had the advantages of decent social surroundings for a generation or two are entirely satisfactory companions." But he also noted another type of Jewish student, those who "had not had the social advantages of their more fortunate fellows" and whose ambition alone brought them to even consider higher education: "Some of these are not particularly pleasant companions, but the total number is not great, and every reputable institution aspiring to public service must stand ready to give to those of probity and good moral character the benefits which they are making great sacrifices to obtain."[10]

These words were uncharacteristically frank even for that faraway world of 1914, and they were written in defense of

---

9. Daniel Bell, *The Reforming of General Education: The Columbia College Experience in Its National Setting* (New York: Anchor Doubleday, 1968), p. 19.

10. Frederick Paul Keppel, *Columbia* (New York: Oxford University Press, 1914), pp. 179, 180.

bringing into the otherwise genteel student body of Columbia College a group we would today call "socially disadvantaged" or "underserved." But Keppel's words reek with anti-Semitism. And in any case, they did not satisfy those who were worried about Columbia's so-called "Jewish Problem." Along with many of its peers, in the 1920s and '30s, Columbia began to strictly limit the number of such "socially undesirable" candidates. In 1928, Columbia even opened the Seth Low Junior College in Brooklyn—a second undergraduate school with, technically, the same admissions requirements as Columbia College, but that, in effect, worked as an overflow catch basin for qualified applicants, permitting the main campus at Morningside to enforce an admissions quota for Jewish students.[11]

More than sixty years after the struggle to contain the influx of Jewish students, I did not arrive at Columbia with the advantages of what Dean Keppel meant by "decent social surroundings for a generation or two." I was definitely the *other* kind of student, and though a gentile, like the man said, probably not a "particularly pleasant companion" for many of my Columbia College peers.

I had been admitted to Columbia through the Higher Education Opportunity Program (HEOP), an always embattled New York State program that partners with colleges to provide financial aid—including a cash stipend to subsidize the purchase of books—to students who meet mixed criteria of financial need and academic under-preparedness. I met both criteria by wide margins. With a still shaky command of English and far from recovered from the shock of immigration, I showed up at Columbia in 1991 for the six-week summer "bridge" program that

---

11. See Robert McCaughey, "Jews at Columbia," ch. 9 in *Stand, Columbia: A History of Columbia University* (New York: Columbia University Press, 2003).

would round off my academic and social preparation for Columbia College. The HEOP program was the contemporary embodiment of the "public service" Keppel demanded of every "reputable institution" in 1914. There I was at Columbia, one of *those* students. Waiting for me and for my cohort of about thirty HEOP students was Literature Humanities: "Sing, goddess, the anger of Peleus' son Achilleus."

Many years later, I would come to teach this course at Columbia, first as a graduate student and then as a non-tenure-track faculty member fresh out of graduate school. It was striking to me that while the HEOP students were, as a rule, easy to pick out in September, by the following May they were not so recognizable. As a teacher of Introduction to Contemporary Civilization, the sophomore analogue to Lit Hum that examines texts in moral and political philosophy, I have continued to observe the progress of HEOP students with care and interest. By the end of their sophomore year, they tend to be indistinguishable from the rest of the student body in academic sophistication. And when I run into them as alumni, I sometimes can't remember if they were HEOP students or not.

o o o

I entered the Columbia campus through the Amsterdam gates in mid-July 1991 with my belongings in an old suitcase. My brother Keysi drove me in the used but faithful Mercury Lynx he had acquired not long before, with Mom and my little brother Ray tagging along. In some ways, I hadn't gone far from home—I could get on the subway and go back to Queens at any time. And yet when Keysi left me at the front desk in John Jay Hall and I took the elevator to the thirteenth floor, I felt as if I had leapt into an abyss. It was one of a handful of moments in my life when I felt completely disarticulated, out of joint, over-whelmed by a feeling of exposure and loneliness. "What the hell am I doing here?" "Where am I?" "I want to go home." If there had been cell phones back then, I might well have called Keysi to ask him to come back and get me.

Earlier that morning, I had gone to the Woolworth's on 99th Street in Corona, Queens, with my cousin Rick to buy some last-minute supplies for my pilgrimage. Rick, in his inspired way, had picked out a blue bandana from a rack and, with an air of ceremony, presented it to me as a going-away present. I wrapped it around my head right there, puffed my chest out, and we both burst into laughter. Everything about that morning felt ordinary, like it was just another day and I was only getting ready to take some clothes to the laundromat. The world was shifting from under me, but it would have been too much for me to see it. Looking back, the emphatic ordinariness of how I felt that morning seems suspect; it was entirely out of tune with what was happening, resolutely out of tune. Not until I said goodbye to Mom, Keysi, and Ray did I begin to grasp that fact that I had once again stepped into a world that felt discontinuous with everything I knew.

The night before, after I had gone to bed at home, Dulce, Rick's mom, had knocked on my door and given me an envelope with eighty dollars in it. She had collected it from family and friends. It was their send-off, and it was Dulce's special way of acknowledging what was about to happen. It would not have occurred to anyone else to do something like that. In fact, everyone seemed pretty indifferent to what was happening. None of us quite understood the meaning of packing up a suitcase and going off to college, and no one had ever heard of the Ivy League. But Dulce understood that that night, my last night on that bed, in that apartment, in that community, was not an ordinary night in my life. She brought me a gift that was also an aspiration and a recognition.

It was only a few years ago that the memory of Dulce knocking on my door that night came back to me, setting off a flood of tears. How could I have forgotten that profound gesture? Why had I forgotten it? And why was I remembering it just then? It was not the first time, nor the last, that some random trigger, without a reason I can discern, exposes me to a high-voltage memory. A memory that was invisible before, but which has all along been exerting a subterranean force, like the massive objects beneath the surface of the moon that astronomers detected because of the gravitational distortions they produced. Each of these memories is a kind of riddle, a cryptic message from belowdecks, an oracle that speaks a truth I have not wanted to know but which has now managed to break through to the surface.

I arrived on campus with Dulce's envelope in my pocket, and that envelope signified something I did not want to face— something I was going to forget and that I would not remember until many years later, when the precariousness of my life was no longer so obvious or so threatening.

I had applied only to colleges in New York City. I could not stomach another uprooting, another dislocation to an alien world. But here I was, standing in this dorm room, with a suitcase, alone, and having nothing to do, and nothing to say, and nowhere to be. How was I to fill the hours before the orientation later that day that would begin to give shape to this situation? For now, there was a vacuum in the pit of my stomach. From my window, I stared at the empty campus of a summer Sunday—the South Lawn, Low Library, the enthroned statue of Alma Matter looking vaguely in my direction, the bells of Riverside Church ringing loud but hollow to my ears.

Without unpacking, I went back downstairs and took a walk around the campus. The sadness and sense of loss began to lift gradually, and by the time the orientation started, I was basically fine. But the episode left a mark. If I experienced anything like that today, I would call it a panic attack.

○ ○ ○

HEOP was enormously helpful in introducing me to the intensity of college classes and, in particular, to the deficiencies in my writing. It also familiarized me with the Columbia campus, introduced me to various administrative services, and brought me close to a cohort of students who, like me, were starting Columbia as its poorest and most "at risk" students. These were considerable benefits that made the bewildering first weeks of college more manageable.

On the other hand, the program made me feel marked, branded in some uncomfortable way. Over the course of the summer, I was often reminded that my admission to Columbia was not a done deal, that it was contingent on successful completion of the summer program. In addition to preparing us academically, the program seemed designed as a test of our trustworthiness. There were strict rules about how far we could stray from campus: we could not go beyond the rectangle between 125th and 110th streets, and between Morningside and Riverside Drives. There was a curfew, and residential counselors would knock on doors each night to make sure we were in our rooms. There were arbitrary constraints on our behavior that seemed to have no other purpose than to test our compliance. It was as if we had to prove our manageability before we would be allowed to be real Columbia students. I found the constant surveillance humiliating. Despite explicit affirmations to the contrary, the underlying message I registered was unmistakable: we didn't *really* belong at Columbia.

It is tempting to frame my summer experience in terms of racism, elitism, and historical exclusion. But it's not that straightforward. The people who organized and ran the summer program were all people of color—some of them HEOP alumni themselves. Broadly speaking, they shared the background of the students they were preparing to enter college. I don't think that we would have tolerated the treatment we received unless it had been coming from people who, clearly, were our strongest advocates and supporters. They were giving us what they felt we needed most, often informed by their own experience as first-generation, low-income students in elite college environments. They had placed bets on us and were determined to instill the almost military discipline that is required of people with our backgrounds to succeed in places like Columbia. Perhaps they understood that the best weapon we had against the "disadvantages" that the six-week program was meant to address was a willingness to deny ourselves what others enjoyed as a matter of course. The world ahead of us would be a test of our capacity to endure the psychic pain of social dislocation. I still don't think that their approach was the right one, but my sense of grievance over the experience has softened over the years.

Since the time I was an undergraduate, a lot has changed in the way that elite colleges treat and support their low-income and first-generation students. But serious problems persist, some with no easy solutions. My summer experience illustrates some of the complexities: the program gave me tools I sorely needed, but it also drove home my outsider status.

Today, "inclusion" and "belonging" are the watchwords for campus programs focused on students with "marginalized identities." But belonging is a funny thing. People don't feel like they belong because they are *told* that they belong. Belonging is among the things that must necessarily go without saying. Explicit institutional gestures at inclusion almost always backfire. Yet gestures must be made. Getting them right is no small challenge, but a challenge that must be met.

The undergraduate college is a potent tool for counteracting the social and economic stratification that the American free-enterprise system generates.[12] When a college doesn't aggressively advance this mission, it becomes another mechanism for reproducing and reinforcing social privilege.

o o o

One of the ways in which colleges can strengthen their leveling function is by organizing general education curricula that equip students for civic life and social agency. Many people today, even academics, take the approach to liberal education based on the study of classics to be elitist and exclusivist, with little understanding of the democratizing impulse behind it, or the democratizing function it continues to serve—not only for students like me, who desperately needed an introduction to the tools of public discourse and action, but for all college students.

We do minority students an unconscionable disservice when we steer them away from the traditional liberal arts curriculum—yet that is, all too often, what we are doing. We condescend to them when we assume that only works in which they find their ethnic or cultural identities affirmed can really illuminate their human experience. Contemporary life today is no less saturated

---

12. Perhaps the obvious also needs to be said here: that pre-K–12 education is a far more important and critical tool for addressing social stratification. As a society, we should be ashamed of the failing of our public school system to live up to the values of equal opportunity and fairness that we claim to stand for.

with the concepts, traditions, institutions, and norms whose historical development is charted in the Core Curriculum than it was in the early 1990s, or in the early 1900s. Today, too, and for all students, a Core education serves a leveling function, sharpening their historical awareness of how the world has come to be what it is, giving them a shared vocabulary with which to describe and act upon it, and equipping them to communicate with others who bring different backgrounds and perspectives to the conversation.

o o o

In late January of my first year of college, the Lit Hum syllabus reached Saint Augustine's *Confessions*. As with every other text we had read in the class, except for Genesis and the gospels, I had no idea what to expect.

Confessions is the story of Saint Augustine's journey to Christian conversion. He opens the book with several pages of artfully strung Biblical quotations in which he wonders by what means he could address himself to such a being as God. There is an earnest anxiety about his project: to explain to God, who already knows and who has given him the very power of expression, how it was that he came to Him. This zero-point in the narrative, before even his birth, is full of tautology and paradox, as if Augustine is spinning in place, unable to launch the telling of his story. But there is also a tender vulnerability and sincerity that, for me, would become the key to a profound sense of recognition: "Who will grant me that you come to my heart and intoxicate it?" and "What am I to you that you command me to love you and that, if I fail to love you, you are angry with me?"[13]

13. Saint Augustine, *Confessions*, Henry Chadwick, trans. (Oxford: Oxford University Press, 2008), I.v.5, p. 5.

But on that first reading, Augustine began to lose me not long after his introductory excursus, with a description of what he calls the "sins of my infancy." He uses the term "infancy" in its literal meaning: *in-fant,* that is, something lacking speech. He acknowledges he doesn't remember that time of his life, but his observation of infants, he says, gives him the information he needs to confess the sins of his own infancy. He sees in babies' "greedy cries for milk" and, in their becoming "vehemently indignant" (9) at not getting what they want, the marks of a diseased will, a sinful nature irresistibly driven by a need to make others "bow to my will" (10). "When I did not get my way," he says, "I used to be indignant with my seniors for their disobedience and with free people who were not slaves to my interests; and I would revenge myself on them by weeping" (7).

When I first read this, it seemed clear to me that Augustine was making an elementary mistake: he was ascribing to preverbal infants cognitive processes, such as premeditation and intention, that are symbolically mediated and could not possibly be part of how the infant related to the world. The infant did not *reason*; it did not act with *foresight*; it did not do *this* in order to achieve *that*; it simply acted out an instinctual program of self-preservation. You don't need to know the first thing about evolution to see that. Why was Augustine laboring this improbable point?

There was more in the first pages of the *Confessions* to turn me off:

I have personally watched and studied a jealous baby. He could not yet speak and, pale with jealousy and bitterness, glared at his brother sharing his mother's milk . . . it can hardly be innocence, when the source of milk is flowing richly and abundantly, not to endure a share going to one's blood-brother, who is in profound need, dependent for life exclusively on that one food (9).

Augustine's description of this baby was motivated, it seemed to me, by a blind commitment to the Christian doctrine that declares man inherently depraved and marred by sin from the moment of conception. It's one thing, I thought, to quietly accept this doctrine, and another to go looking at a baby's behavior and ascribe to it vicious and malevolent intention. It seemed to me a sloppy and bad-faith justification for a suspect idea that he had accepted as a matter of faith and which he now tried to advance on the basis of a dubious interpretation of a baby's preconscious behavior. This was an only slightly more sophisticated version of what, growing up in the Dominican Republic, I had seen Christians all around me do. It always irked me. Seeing it in this ancient and revered source, proffered to me by the Columbia faculty as one of the towering achievements of ancient thought, puzzled me. Augustine's reasoning felt dishonest, forced. Was I meant to take this seriously? Or was I reading it as an example of how blind faith can turn even a "great" thinker into a simpleminded fanatic?

Yet despite this disconcerting opening riff on the sins of infancy, *Confessions* had an enormous impact on me, and for a few weeks, it even revived my sense of Christianity as a possible way of life. In Augustine, I found many echoes of my own experience. His acceptance of Christianity after a long period of rejection and ridicule reminded me of my own conversion of a few years before; his relationship with Ambrose echoed my own with Ernesto Cervantes, who would become my pastor; his discovery that the version of Christianity he had mocked in his youth was not the only one possible; his evolution from denier, to skeptic, to convert; his earnest neediness; his restless intellect; his insatiable curiosity . . . all of these things resonated deeply with me and made me recognize in Augustine an intimate kin, a writer who seemed to understand something elusive about my own inner life, and whose honesty and devotion disarmed me.

As a College freshman, I was desperately trying to make sense of the strange and dislocated life I was living, trying to find some footing in the disorienting world in which I found myself. I was trying to understand the path that had led me to evangelical Christianity in high school and, at the same time, painfully relinquishing its certainties and emotional comforts. I was trying to determine who I was and what I was to become.

At eighteen, unmoored from my relatives in Queens, from the church I had helped Ernesto start, from my childhood life in the Dominican Republic, and from my parents, I was urgently trying to get a fix on myself, to find some anchored center of identity. I had landed at John F. Kennedy International airport in New York City in May 1985, two days before my twelfth birthday, not speaking English and having no idea what was to happen to me. I now realize that no one else knew either. If, somehow, you got the chance to immigrate legally to the United States from the Dominican Republic in the mid-1980s, you didn't ask why you should do it or what you would do once you got there. You just did it. And so it was done.

What would happen to me in the US soon began take its anomalous shape: my father, who had accompanied my older brother and me on the trip, would not stay and reunite with my mother to begin a new life in America; he would return to the Dominican Republic and live his life there, with the family he had made after he and Mom had divorced when I was five. My mother, ill-equipped to navigate the complexities of life in New York, where she had now lived for three years, would be fired from her minimum-wage factory job in Brooklyn and take up with a man my brother and I did not trust and with whom we refused live. Instead, we would live in a room in the basement of Juan and Fefa Alcántara's house, making do as best we could. We would take meals with the large Alcántara family. My brother would get a job as a security guard in a department store and would contribute almost everything he made to the household's expenses.

My father and his very Pentecostal cousin, Fefa, were not especially close. Only formally friendly, actually. But he was lifelong friends with Fefa's husband, Juan, and had played, back in Cambita, a key role in facilitating the desperate young love of Juan, his friend, and Fefa, his cousin. No explicit agreement about money was reached with respect to our moving into Fefa's house, only what was understood among friends and kindred from a world that was, even in the mid-'80s, a throwback to a different age. In that old world, mutual obligations were exactly those things that didn't need to be specified. The person in need would not ask for help; the person giving it would not mention it. But there was no denying that we were going to be what Dominicans call *arrimados*—not quite guests and not quite boarders, but something in between: refugees dependent on the acceptance of a familial obligation by the host.

So it was that in the space of a few months, even as my pituitary gland began to transform my body into that of an adolescent, the life I had lived until then had transmuted into something I could not understand. And so it was that I became ripe for religion.

It happened just at this time, as my brother and I were added to a large roster of mouths to feed and children to mind in Fefa's household, that the whole family was being convulsed by a religious awakening. And while my brother resisted, I was swept along: I let go the soft atheism that my father, my reason, and the fanaticism of the people I knew who called themselves Christians had engendered in me, and gave myself over to the new and wonderful sweetness of salvation.

The variety of Christianity that had swept the household and replaced the austere Pentecostalism brought from the Dominican Republic used to be called "Word of Faith" and has a solid pedigree of charismatic, tongue-talking, miracle-working, prosperity-touting American apostles. But it was not these aspects—which always seemed a little suspect to me—that drew me in. It was, first and foremost, Ernesto Cervantes, the warmhearted and magnetic messenger who brought the new gospel. The new revelation rejected the self-righteous severity and narrow-mindedness of the backwoods Pentecostalism I had known in DR. It suggested that a life of faith was actually compatible with reason.

The message came to Fefa's household and revolutionized it. The new and vibrant understanding of Christianity caused a rift with the local Pentecostal church, of which the family had been a founding pillar. In the new movement, there was also a flavor of rebellion. It was exhilarating to see Ernesto extricate the family from the dogmatism of the old doctrines. And he did so with charm, warmth, and intelligence I had never seen in a believer.

Ernesto, a brilliant close reader, began to visit the house on Monday nights to offer Bible studies. I started attending them out of politeness, but it gradually turned into genuine interest. He took note of my attentiveness and curiosity. He invited me to his daughter's birthday party. He took my questions seriously and had answers, good answers, to every issue I raised—about God's foreknowledge and our free will, about internal contradictions in the Bible that I had grown up hearing my father expound on, about Christianity's complicity in imperialism, about religion as "the opium of the masses."

Ernesto's personal interest and nourishing attention—and the new panoramas that his vision of Christianity offered—were irresistible to me. Being singled out for attention was irresistible. Being seen was irresistible. Before long, I was in shoes much like Augustine's in Milan under the influence of Ambrose's preaching: "More and more my conviction grew that all the knotty problems and clever calumnies which those deceivers of ours had devised against the divine books could be dissolved."[14]

My newfound faith brought many happy days to my life and accelerated my learning of English by daily, devoted, and absorbed reading of the King James Version of the Bible. In Fefa's house, I was no longer a heathenish burden, but a miraculous blessing and testament to the power of the new message. My conversion brought light into the family, made me closer to Fefa's children, and took away, temporarily, my feeling of being a stranger in an alien world. We prayed together, we sang together, we went to church together.

All of this was with me, fresh with me, as I encountered Saint Augustine's *Confessions* in January 1992. *Confessions* is an intensely intimate book, and you always have the sense that you have just walked into a private, whispered conversation. The book invites you to witness a probing, urgent heart-to-heart between Augustine and his God. The subject is Augustine himself; the journey of becoming Augustine. The object of attention is the self. It is Augustine's self-analysis.

We probably know more about the psychology and inner life of Saint Augustine than that of any other ancient person. Before

---

14. *Confessions*, VI.iii.4, p. 93.

conversion, he was a prominent teacher of rhetoric, so in his self-exploration, and in the telling of his life story, he had at his disposal an unsurpassed range of rhetorical tools. His expressive capacity—in particular, his skill at describing emotion and inner experience—is unlike anyone else before modernity.

The first few books of *Confessions* are slow, and one can get annoyed at what feels like Augustine's gratuitous beatings around the bush, his reliance on Biblical quotations to say even the most commonplace things, his distracted curiosity that seems unable to stay on any subject. Here's how the second paragraph of the book starts: "Grant me Lord to know and understand (Ps. 118:34, 73, 144) which comes first—to call upon you or to praise you, and whether knowing you precedes calling on you. But who calls upon you when he does not know you? For an ignorant person might call upon someone else instead of the right one. But surely you may be called upon in prayer that you may be known" (3) . . . and on, and on, and on. It can be exasperating. Especially if you are reading quickly, as I was in Lit Hum. But once I got past that difficult entry, Augustine had his hooks in me. His insights into human psychology were illuminating and profound, and came to me in a language I understood.

Teaching the book to Columbia first-year students many years later, I found that my transformative first encounter with the text is the exception rather than the rule for the typical eighteen-year-old. Many students find it hard to establish the sympathetic bond that must undergird any powerful encounter with a work of literature. This bond is hard to form for students with Augustine, I think, for reasons embedded in our post-Christian and postmodern condition. It's hard, in our post-faith world, to inhabit the mind of someone who lives with a vivid sense of God's presence. I even find some of my students reluctant to admit to a sincere longing for truth, and to the possibility of truth, because it is intellectually unfashionable.

Teaching the *Confessions* in Lit Hum involves facilitating this affective extension for the student, a process that, like all humanities teaching, is partly mysterious and happens more by contagion from one mind to another than by explicit instruction. What makes humanities pedagogy effective is the instructor's capacity to animate what might be alien to the student and evoke, from what might at first look like a carcass, a vital and compelling voice.

That's why the teacher, in his or her person, is so crucial to the liberal arts classroom. Especially in first-year seminars, the teacher makes or breaks the class. In my early years as Director of the Center for the Core Curriculum at Columbia, my associate director, Janine de Novais, who had herself gone through the Core as an undergraduate, rose in a faculty meeting discussing the experience of minority students in the Core classroom and made a statement that, I thought, deserved to be engraved and displayed in some prominent place: "If the Core is not taught well, the Core is not taught."

Janine's dictum points to the fact that it is not the list of works read in a Core course that determines whether a student of color or an international student or a poor student feels excluded or in some way alienated. The decisive factor is the way those texts are taught and the atmosphere that the instructor creates in the classroom. And Janine's point holds true beyond the experience of minority students. Inspired and skilled teaching is a constitutive component of liberal education. It is not an add-on or a perk; without it, a liberal education simply does not happen. "If the Core is not taught well, the Core is not taught." For good and ill, liberal education is a personality-driven enterprise, and only through an intensely personal and, in some special way, intimate bond between the teacher and student can the task be accomplished.

John Erskine's reflection on what his General Honors course required of a teacher holds true for liberal education in general:

> Unless great books are our very life, unless we look forward hungrily to the next opportunity to read them ourselves or to hear our students discuss them, unless by impulse and choice we are turning them over in our mind as we walk across campus or through the school hallways, it is only a cold dish we are likely to serve up to our pupils, and they, taking their cue from us, will discuss great and noble ideas at low temperature and on a low plane.[15]

The work of liberal education cannot be done without a personal investment in the task, it cannot be done by routine, it cannot be faked, and it cannot be mass-produced. In the "Divinity School Address," Ralph Waldo Emerson spoke of the role of the preacher in terms directly applicable to the liberal arts professor. "The true preacher," he said, "can be known by this, that he deals out to the people his life,—life passed through the fire of thought."[16] The liberal arts teacher, as it were, casts sparks with his or her own intellectual activity before the student. Some of these sparks land on dry kindling and start a fire that is the students' own.

As a college freshman, my own religious experiences gave me an advantage, an entry point, into Augustine that others did not have. The power of his mind, the beauty of his language, and the

---

15. *My Life as a Teacher*, p. 171.

16. Ralph Waldo Emerson, *Selections from Ralph Waldo Emerson: An Organic Anthology*, Stephen Whicher, ed. (Boston: Houghton Mifflin, 1960), p. 109.

depth of insight that pervades his writing captivated me. In plumbing the depths of his own psyche, Augustine gave me a language with which to approach my own interiority; he gave me a model and a set of questions with which to explore the emotional wilderness, full of doubt and confusion, that was my own coming-to-adulthood, in America, in New York City, at Columbia. Perhaps what most amazed me about the saint was his consciousness that his own heart was a mystery, that its inner recesses were dark, unknown, and often inaccessible. Yet he was relentlessly committed to burrowing deeper and deeper into his own self and to discovering there, in the end, the only form of truth he would accept. Far from a pedantic or doctrinaire holy man, I found an uncertain, childlike man trying desperately to make sense of his own being in the world.

o o o

Augustine possessed not only a restless intellect but a sensual and passionate personality. One of his favorite words throughout the *Confessions* is "sweetness" (*suavitas*). He is keenly attuned to pleasure—spiritual, intellectual, and carnal. The big impediment to his conversion, for example, was giving up sex. Throughout his writings, of which *Confessions* is only a tiny portion, the fleshy pleasures and torments of human life are a constant object of inquiry and theological speculation. His writing illustrates that an obsession with pleasure is the true mark of an ascetic. It is not those least sensible to pleasure who choose the life of abstinence, but those most susceptible to its allure, like the alcoholics who must give up drink altogether precisely because they like it so much. So Augustine, like all ascetics, had a strong weakness for pleasure, and he continually highlights the spiritual pleasures and ecstasies of his chosen life of abstinence. It struck me vividly that Augustine had not, in fact, given up pleasure when taking up celibacy and other monastic rigors. Instead, he traded one kind of pleasure for another. His was not a life of dry monotony and arid isolation, but one full of inner drama, adventure, and life-expanding discoveries.

In the final analysis, though, Augustine's strongest attachment was to truth and to the possibility of attaining it. There is, in the *Confessions*, an overriding epistemological urgency: to find out the truth and to live according to it. The energy of the book comes from an anxiety to *know*, to find a place of intellectual anchoring. In Augustine's words: "My concern to discover what I could hold for certain gnawed at my vitals,"[17] and "our heart is restless until it rests in you."[18] That's how it was for him. And that's an impulse that touched some deep core within me as well.

The climax of the *Confessions* comes in July 386 in Augustine's house in Milan. He and his close friend Alypius have received a surprise visit from another African émigré named Ponticianus who, like Augustine and Alypius, had achieved reasonable success in the complex social hierarchies of late imperial Rome. Ponticianus had recently converted to Christianity after reading *The Life of Antony*, a biography of the Egyptian monk, who, in part because of this biography, written by Athanasius of Alexandria, became a major figure in Christian monasticism. Finding and reading the book while on a leisurely walk with a colleague, Ponticianus was overwhelmed by its appeal to a life of complete devotion to God. Augustine writes:

---

17. *Confessions*, VI.iii.5, p. 94.
18. *Confessions*, I.i.1, p. 3.

Suddenly, he was filled with holy love and sobering shame. Angry with himself, he turned his eyes on his friend and said to him: "Tell me, I beg you, what do we hope to achieve with our labors? What is our aim in life? What is the motive of our service to the state?"[19]

On the margin of my book in 1992, I wrote next to this passage: "The Questions." These seemed to me to be indeed The Questions. They still do. Boiled down to one, it is, "What is worth striving for?" This is the question of the life of a free person, the question that freedom of action and pursuit ineluctably raises. It is the question that liberal education continually asks.

In liberal democracies, where personal freedom is the guiding political value, this ancient question confronts the individual with special force. This isn't to deny the fact that, in liberal democracies, people's actual choices are often severely constrained and that the dream of personal freedom is for many just that, a dream. But it's also true that for many, and I among them, modern life affords a degree of freedom to shape one's own destiny that would have been inconceivable at any other time in history. Coming to the US just as I entered adolescence dramatically expanded that freedom. The world lay in front of me full of strange and unimaginable possibilities. What do I hope to achieve with my labors? What was my aim in life? What was the purpose of my striving?

Ponticianus's conversion is the trigger to the climactic moment of the *Confessions*, when Augustine breaks down under a fig tree in the garden of his house in Milan and the grace of God pours over him. As with Ponticianus, the moment of conversion is midwifed by a text—in this case, the words of the Apostle

---

19. *Confessions*, VIII.vi.15, p. 143.

Paul admonishing believers to give up riots and drunken parties, eroticism and indecencies, strife and rivalry, and to "put ye
on the Lord Jesus Christ, and make not provision for the flesh,
to fulfil the lusts thereof."[20]

Augustine was my first glimpse at—my first experience
of—a spirituality that felt genuine. It did not reinforce any specific belief, but it deepened me. I read Augustine. I gorged on
Augustine. Theological questions of the deepest order and of
which my mind had only the slightest suspicion became, suddenly, dazzling revelations. Here was a mind unafraid of asking
and asking and asking and unwilling to settle for anything that
did not both persuade his reason and satisfy his heart.

I saw things about the world in Augustine that I had never
seen before. I saw things about myself and about the kind of life
that, it had begun to seem, was really worthwhile living. I saw
in Augustine that I must leave the evangelical faith and the
church for good, perhaps for a different atheism than the one I
came to America with, or perhaps for a higher sort of faith, one
that grew from the soil of utter intellectual honesty. I did not
know where I would go, but I had been re-oriented and somehow clarified, somehow acquainted with the terms on which I
would count my life as authentic. I had seen the possibility of a
life of intellectual integrity that still grappled, honestly, with the
mysteries of living. In Augustine, I had seen the possibility of
reconciling my deepest hunger for truth with my growing perception of its stubborn elusiveness.

My first year in college breathed a kind of new life into me.
It placed my own personal experience in a larger, even cosmic,
context. And while Augustine didn't exactly revive my faith in

---

20. *Confessions*, VIII.xii.29, p. 153, echoing Romans 13:13–14 (King James
Version).

God, it revived my faith in my own experience, it dignified and legitimized my tryst with Christianity, and affirmed my deepest impulses toward a life dedicated to the pursuit of an ultimate good. "This was the story Ponticianus told. But while he was speaking, Lord, you turned my attention back to myself. You took me up from behind my own back where I had placed myself because I did not wish to observe myself (Ps. 20:13), and you placed me before my face (Ps. 49:21)." "Little by little, Lord, with a most gentle and merciful hand you touched and calmed my heart."[21]

I have now lived with Augustine for almost thirty years, as a reader and as a teacher. Even what initially struck me as Augustine's dogmatic and narrow-minded judgment of a baby's cry for milk now appears in a different light. Like much else in the strange old books I was reading in the Columbia Core Curriculum, Augustine's sometimes jarring observations would prove to hold more water than I first suspected.

o o o

I had had an innocent childhood in my small town at the foot of big mountains in the Dominican Republic: Cambita Garabitos. Cambita extended six streets in one direction and four in the other. My address, recorded into my young memory like an incantation, was *calle seis, casa siete*: the seventh house on the sixth street. Today, all the streets have names, and the town has spawned neighborhoods on the edges that are themselves larger than the original grid in which I grew up. Roads were paved at some point when I was very young; I have hazy memories of trucks, gravel, the hot smell of tar, and giant rollers. The big

---

21. *Confessions*, VIII.vii.16, p. 144; *Confessions*, VI.v.7, p. 95.

machines that rumbled into town were by far the most amazing sight any of us kids had ever seen. At some other point in my childhood, we got semi-reliable running water—I remember my father, during some period, often going with a "brigade" to work on an "aqueduct," and one day there was an inauguration ceremony and water coming out of a faucet in the kitchen. There was one gas station in Cambita, which contained the town's one telephone. You would pick it up and wait. Eventually, a lady operator would say something on the other side. Then you told her the number you wanted to call.

I was allowed to run everywhere I pleased. And I ran a lot, near naked, along unpaved streets and dusty paths, stealing fruit from neighbors' trees, though never followed by the kinds of pangs that tormented Augustine after a famous incident with pears. I would venture to the hills for even finer fruity delicacies. At home, there was no television, no stove, no refrigerator, and no phone. Sometimes, as a shorthand, I simply say that I grew up in the nineteenth century among people who had grown up in the eighteenth.

There was a lot of violence around—a kind of savage, naked, almost casual violence. People would kill each other with machetes. Teenage lovers would drink poison. Husbands would murder their wives. Kids would drown. Amateur electricians would die electrocuted, their heels bursting open from the high voltage. Friends, after a night drinking and playing dominoes, would be possessed by demonic rage and fight until one killed the other. But this grown-up violence would never reach me directly. It felt real, but always at a distance, like those people you heard about on the radio every Sunday who had won the national lottery.

There were also a lot of babies around. My father is one of twelve, my mother one of five. So I had ten thousand first and second cousins of all ages and description. In my own household, from Dad's second marriage (I call it a marriage, but there were no papers officializing the union), there were two babies in the house: my sister Ruth, who was five when I left for New York, and my brother Lewis, who was two. In Fefa's house in New York, there had also been a lot of babies. Dilcia (Fefa's sister) and Secundino's baby. Moisés and Luli's two babies. Cousin Ruth's baby. Noemí's and Chuíto's babies. Milciades (Fefa's brother) and Dulce's baby (they lived around the corner).

And then, my little brother Ray, born in the South Bronx, who was one when my brother Keysi and I engineered renting an apartment down the street from Fefa's house during my sophomore year of high school. We rented the apartment by teaming up with an acquaintance from Cambita who was living in a rented room nearby. My brother Keysi carried the main burden of our share of the rent, and I contributed what I had saved from a summer job to the initial rent deposit. Almost immediately, I became very close to Ray, watching and raising him with a sort of desperate attentiveness and kindliness—trying to correct, as I now realize, the deficiencies and cruelties I ascribed to my older brother.

So I felt I knew babies pretty well when I encountered Augustine's ruminations. And I knew he was wrong about them, even though so much else in the *Confessions* felt right. Yet Augustine was a teacher of rhetoric, the art of persuasion. Somewhere along the way, I began to suspect that he knew full well what he was up to in his description of infants and that there was something I wasn't seeing. Could my initial impression of his doctrinaire naïveté be right? Or was my quick judgment itself naïve?

o o o

Augustine's move from infancy to childhood, the crucial transition from pre-verbal to verbal, had caught my full attention. I think I had always been attuned to language (I have an early memory, before going to school, of realizing, like a flash, how consonants and vowels came to gather to represent sound, which unlocked, in a single stroke, the mystery of writing). But my coming to America at twelve and learning English with full awareness of what was happening turned language-learning into a special preoccupation for me. I felt that, even without any theoretical knowledge, I had special insight into the process of language acquisition. This is how Augustine describes it:

> On the path to the present, I emerged from infancy to boyhood, or rather boyhood came upon me and succeeded infancy. Infancy did not "depart," for it has nowhere to go. Yet I was no longer a baby incapable of speech but already a boy with power to talk. This I remember. But how I learned to talk I discovered only later. It was not that grown-up people instructed me by presenting me with words in a certain order by formal teaching, as later I was to learn the letters and alphabet. I myself acquired this power of speech with the intelligence which you gave me, my God. By groans and various sounds and various movements of parts of my body I would endeavor to express the intentions of my heart to persuade people to bow to my will.[22]

How time passes and how it brings about that one thing becomes another is a constant fascination for Augustine. He dedicates one of the last books of the *Confessions*—once he's done telling his personal story—to a mind-bending philosophical exploration of the nature of time—the medium in which his

---

22. *Confessions*, I.vii.13, p. 10.

life, and all of creation, unfolds. In this passage, he hints at a phenomenon so strange and yet so pervasive that we hardly notice it: that the present emerges from the past, as if it was contained in it. That metaphor fails because time is not a material substance, but one is at pains to describe what other kind of thing it is.

In any case, one state succeeds another: we were infants without speech, without the power of memory, and gradually we emerge from "the darkness of forgetfulness" (10), into the light of awareness and memory. Where did we emerge from and where did that time go? At what point did we cross the threshold of awareness and memory, and where and what was one before that? Or was awareness and the power to remember a gradual illumination, like the rising of dawn, with no discernible point of origin? Looking back into my early childhood, memories are blurry and episodic until gradually, around the age of five, a thread of memory becomes distinct, one which I can roughly follow until the present (I remember precisely because the day this thread of memory starts is the day I woke up in my aunt's house, my parents having had their final fight the night before and separating forever).

Augustine's rumination about infant language acquisition in this passage shows the sophistication of his understanding. It was not that the grown-ups instructed him, but that he himself acquired the power of speech "with the intelligence which you [God] gave me." Augustine is pointing to a kind of mystery in how children learn language. The speed and accuracy with which infants learn complex meanings and grasp deep grammatical structures suggests an inbuilt predisposition in a child to spawn, as it were, a complex and rule-governed language system after exposure to a relatively limited regimen of linguistic priming.

Noam Chomsky took this idea and ran with it, transforming and in many ways creating the field of linguistics by introducing the revolutionary idea of a universal grammar that is shared by all human languages and which humans are predisposed to intuit by virtue of the biological architecture of their brain. Understanding this uniquely human endowment, the "language faculty," is as promising an approach to understanding "human nature" as any conceived by modern science. Figuring out all we can about this underlying language faculty became the Chomskyan project and continues to generate surprising insights.

Plato had already put this notion in the air with the Socratic theory that all knowledge is recollection—that when you "learn" something, you are merely remembering, or making explicit, what you already knew. In a dramatic demonstration of this in the dialogue *Meno*, Socrates has a slave boy solve a difficult geometrical problem by responding to his simple questions. Socrates uses the demonstration to show that, in some sense, the slave already "knew" the answer but had not realized that he knew it. All Socrates had to do was direct his attention to knowledge he already possessed. Similarly, Augustine learns language not from adult instruction but "with the intelligence which you gave me, my God."

Reading Augustine and other ancients, as I do with undergraduates, is a sort of archeological exercise. Much of what seems strange and remote has, in fact, a genealogical relation to how we understand the world today. Spending time with these ideas and perspectives deepens our understanding of the contemporary world by revealing how what we think today emerges from and is shaped by discarded foundations. Ancient articles of faith, for instance, like ancient myths, may strike us as simplistic and misguided, at odds with our own perceptions and certainties. Yet they often contain deep human truths, even if clothed in language we no longer understand or grounded on metaphysical assumptions we no longer share. But like the archeologist, with care and interest, we can recover some of the ancient understandings and use them to enrich and add texture to contemporary knowledge. Such an exercise has the salutary effect of sowing a little doubt in our own certainties, reminding us that we, too, are historically circumscribed. So with the ancients—and with anyone, really—before a dismissal of what seems patently wrong, it is worth asking, "In what way are they right?"

Take the most theologically consequential sentence in Augustine's description of language acquisition: "By groans and various sounds and various movements of parts of my body I would endeavor to express the intentions of my heart *to persuade people to bow to my will*" (emphasis added). Augustine detects the inveterate urge to dominate and to bend others to our will shining through the acquisition of language. Just as innate as the capacity to learn language is a proclivity to assert the prerogatives of self above all other considerations. This incorrigible crook in the human heart stains even our most well-meaning actions and insinuates itself into our best intentions. Even as infants. This is the doctrine of original sin.

As a first-year college student, Augustine's full-throttle endorsement of this doctrine of original sin (or innate depravity, as Calvinists liked to call it) was the most difficult thing of all to reconcile with my admiration of his mind and my fascination with the religious life he had chosen. In what way was he right?

As a sophomore, I read some more Augustine, in the second-year Core requirement Introduction to Contemporary Civilization in the West, more commonly known as Contemporary Civilization or simply CC. Like Literature Humanities, CC is a year-long course in "Important Books," this time with a focus on more philosophical works. It is the original course in the Columbia Core Curriculum, formulated with the catastrophe of World War I still fresh in view and first offered in September 1919. It was a course, as Jacques Barzun put it, "born of trauma"[23] and meant to introduce students to the "insistent problems of the present." Originally, the course offered a survey of the latest discoveries in the social sciences as well as the intellectual history of Western institutions from the Middle Ages through to the present. Following the example of its younger sibling Literature Humanities, however, CC evolved, beginning in the 1940s, into a course based on the reading of primary texts in the Western tradition of ethical and political inquiry.

Even after its transformation into what is sometimes called a "great books" course, Contemporary Civilization concerned itself explicitly with the knowledge base that a citizen of America's experiment in self-government ought to command in order to effectively participate in it. For a time, it was a two-year sequence, with the second year dedicated primarily to problems of the American economy. That second-year course was eventually dropped, though its shadow remains in the official name of the remaining course: Introduction to Contemporary Civilization in the West. As the second-year course was abandoned, the first year extended into the present, so that today's course ends with texts and issues of contemporary import, such as intersectionality, mass incarceration, and the postcolonial condition. The course's emphasis on political citizenship and contemporary problems made it, from its conception, a nondisciplinary course. If Literature Humanities can be described

---

23. Unpublished transcript of 1987 talk on the occasion of the 50th anniversary of Literature Humanities.

as a course about what it means to be an individual, Contemporary Civilization can be described as a course about what it means to be a member of a community.

○ ○ ○

As one of the most consequential explorations of political life in antiquity, Augustine's enormous tome *City of God* is a staple of the fall semester of CC. There, I began to see the power of the doctrine of original sin to explain the character of so much that is observable in political life. One anecdote Augustine tells early in the book illustrates his whole view of earthly politics:

> For it was a witty and truthful rejoinder which was given by a captured pirate to Alexander the Great. The king asked the fellow, "What is your idea, in infesting the sea?" And the pirate answered, with uninhibited insolence, "The same as yours, in infesting the earth! But because I do it with a tiny craft, I'm called a pirate; because you have a mighty navy, you're called an emperor."[24]

Augustine makes a grating but astute point about the nature of political power. It felt intuitively true to me. I had grown up experiencing American foreign policy from the point of view of the Latin American left, seeing my father's political heroes deposed, jailed, and hunted down by right-wing authoritarian regimes with the support and encouragement of the United States. My father had cut his political teeth opposing the American invasion of the Dominican Republic in 1965, an invasion meant to prevent the reinstatement of Juan Bosch, a socialist

---

24. Saint Augustine, *Concerning the City of God, against the Pagans,* Henry Bettenson, trans. (London: Penguin Classics, 1984), p. 139.

and Castro-friendly democratically elected President who had suffered a CIA-backed coup d'état in late 1963, after only seven months in power. The strongman installed in his place, Joaquín Balaguer, would dominate Dominican politics for the next thirty years. He was hated in my household, and my father and his political associates were hated in his regime.

I understood early in my life the realpolitik of American Cold War foreign policy and how it was used to justify abuses in Latin America. I saw Dad and his comrades persecuted and harassed by the US-backed government; I saw him go to jail; once, he spent five days in solitary confinement without food or water; I heard of the suspicious deaths of some of his comrades; I knew what it was to be rushed away from the house in the middle of the night for a sudden holiday in the mountains that would happen to coincide with increased police presence in Cambita. *El imperialismo Yanqui* was a norm of international relations with which I was well acquainted.

Only later did I come to see that Dad's admired regimes—in the Soviet bloc, in Africa, in Cuba, the Sandinistas in Nicaragua, and others in the same vein—were playing the same game as the Yanquis, but with fewer guns and smaller boats. Augustine was onto it long ago. His anecdote about the emperor and the pirate is meant to show that the international order is the world of individual human relations written in large letters: a Hobbesian world where the powerful impose their will and where norms of justice are invariably subordinated to the prerogatives of self-interest.

In *City of God*, Augustine distinguishes between the City of God and the City of Man. The City of God is a mystical entity composed of Christians whose lives on earth are a sort of pilgrimage on the way to eternity in God's bosom; the City of Man is the earthly, secular world of unregenerate people, represented most distinctly in Augustine's mind by the Roman Empire. In the process of analyzing and diagnosing the rise and fall of the Roman Empire in *City of God*, Augustine gives us an extended meditation on the nature of human society, government, politics, and history. He aims to show that in the City of Man all human relations are ultimately relations of power: "Because I do it with a tiny craft, I am called a pirate; because you have a mighty navy, you're called an emperor."

Augustine opened a question for me that, once I started asking it, has proved to be extraordinarily fertile: To what extent am I—and others—motivated by an urge to dominate, to impose our will, to subjugate others? To what extent, to use Nietzsche's formulation, is the world nothing but "the will to power"? There is a long line of thinkers, religious and not, who share some version of this view of human life: not only Augustine, Hobbes, and Nietzsche, but Thucydides, Luther, Machiavelli, and Freud. I think of these thinkers as power theorists. Thomas Hobbes put it this way: "So, in the first place, I put for a general inclination of all mankind, a perpetual and restless desire of power after power, that ceaseth only in death."[25] Augustine caused me to consult myself on this question—habitually. To what extent does the urge for power and dominance pervade my actions, thoughts, and choices? Or, to return to Augustine's language, to what extent can I observe original sin in my own constitution?

The doctrine of original sin points to something undeniable about the human condition. It is not just a religious idea, nor the mere prejudice of saints. In fact, this condition has been the object of reflection for thinkers in all ages and in all places. It is

---

25. Thomas Hobbes, *Leviathan* (Oxford and New York: Oxford University Press, 1996), p. 66.

there, notably, in the political philosophy of the framers of the American Constitution, who, in the words of James Madison's famous *Federalist*, no. 51, organized a government in which "ambition must be made to counteract ambition," for "if men were angels, no government would be necessary."[26]

The American theologian Reinhold Niebuhr would call those who, recognizing the condition of original sin, live by its rules "the children of darkness": "moral cynics who know no law beyond their will and interest." The "children of light," on the other hand, "believe that self-interest should be brought under the discipline of a higher law." And with his dry and cutting prescience, he notes that the children of light are afflicted by an endemic naïveté: they are "foolish not merely because they underestimate the power of self-interest among the children of darkness. They underestimate this power among themselves."[27]

Augustine does not seem to share this characteristic gullibility of the children of light, and hence gives us a dark and depressing view of the possibility of justice in our earthly realm, flawed as we are even in our most deliberate judgments, and marred with greed and self-interest as even our best intentions reveal themselves to be on honest inspection.

Late in *City of God*, there's a chapter titled "The Mistakes of Human Judgement, When the Truth Is Hidden," in which Augustine turns his attention explicitly to the administration of justice in the City of Man. His conclusion is that because of lying witnesses, false confessions, ambiguities in the legal process and, ultimately, because of the inherent fallibility of human

---

26. Alexander Hamilton, James Madison, and John Jay, *The Federalist Papers* (New York: Signet Classics, 2003), p. 319.

27. Reinhold Niebuhr, *The Children of Light and the Children of Darkness* (Chicago: University of Chicago Press, 2011), pp. 9, 11.

judgment, earthly justice is, in fact, impossible. "The wise judge does not act in this way through a will to do harm, but because ignorance is unavoidable—and yet the exigencies of human society make judgement also unavoidable. Here we have what I call the wretchedness of man's situation." Human society, in other words, demands the administration of justice, but is incapable of actually delivering it. Such is our misery.[28]

For Augustine, the City of Man is predicated on conquest and subjugation, not justice. The realities of human institutions and human justice are inextricable from our lust for power, our thirst for pleasure, and our incapacity to subordinate the self to a higher law. For him, the defect in Plato, Aristotle, and Cicero—indeed in all pagan political philosophy—is not in the notions of justice, order, and citizenship they uphold, but in their blindness to the utter impossibility of their realization, given the nature of man. The stain of sin and corruption runs too deep for us to organize ourselves along the ideal lines proposed by secular political thinkers. In this life, we are bound to fall short of our own ideals of justice, bound to be unable to live according to reason. In this life, we will need laws, coercion, punishments, and executors—all of which actually negate our pretensions to justice.

This is all hard to swallow. Is there really no possibility of earthly redemption, no salvation based on human effort and decency? Are we irredeemably dammed and condemned to misery in this world—never mind the hereafter—unless saved by supernatural intervention? In what way is Augustine right?

While affirming for me the possibility of a genuine intellectual life, even of a genuine spiritual life, Augustine left no room to do it except by surrendering to a transcendent order and,

---

28. *City of God*, p. 860.

even then, looking to an afterlife for its actual fulfillment. And yet, even in Augustine, we see that man's innate depravity is not all there is to humanity. We also have, as David Hume put it in his *Enquiry Concerning the Principles of Morals*, "some particle of the dove, kneaded into our frame, along with the elements of the wolf and the serpent."[29] As much as we find in ourselves the pervading influence of self-interest and desire for domination, we also find impulses toward, and glimpses of, a different set of tendencies that offset and often check, qualify, and sometimes override the prerogatives of self.[30] Against his own agenda, I read Augustine for the possibility of human virtue, for a vision of a this-worldly life worth living.

As a young man of seventeen, Augustine himself found the thread that leads in this direction. He found it in the study of philosophy. For him, the philosophic search for truth and wisdom became itself a path to God, the path to redemption. In the *Confessions*, he recalls his first encounter with the writings of Cicero as a young man:

> That book contains an exhortation to study philosophy and is entitled *Hortensius*. The book changed my feeling. It altered my prayers, Lord, to be towards yourself. It gave me different values and priorities. Suddenly every vain hope

---

29. David Hume, *An Enquiry Concerning the Principles of Morals* (Indianapolis and Cambridge: Hackett Publishing Company, 1983), p. 74.

30. Adam Smith famously begins his 1759 *Theory of Moral Sentiments* (Cambridge: Cambridge University Press, 2002) with this very point: "How selfish soever man may be supposed, there are evidently some principles in his nature, which interest him in the fortune of others, and render their happiness necessary to him, though he derives nothing from it except the pleasure of seeing it" (11). Free-market models of behavior that presume a purely profit-maximizing agent, though often inspired by Smith's later work, *The Wealth of Nations*, miss something fundamental about Smith's much more nuanced grasp of the sources of human motivation.

became empty to me, and I longed for the immortality of wisdom with an incredible ardor in my heart. I began to rise up and return to you.[31]

By embracing Cicero's exhortation to a philosophic life, "I began to rise up and return to you." Reading this at the start of a journey into a world I could not have imagined and which, to this day, I cannot adequately represent to many of the dearest and closest people in my life, suggested to me, religion aside, a way of life; it held out a human possibility that Augustine himself denies. It spoke to me of a higher path than that of attaining prominence in this or that field, or of achieving the material comforts I had grown up without. There was something even more worthwhile for me to pursue.

o o o

The notion that the end goal of learning is God is an old and powerful idea. Instead of "God," others, like Plato and Aristotle, might call it the Supreme Good, or simply, as Gandhi did, Truth. In Plato, education, philosophic education, was the way forward on this path:

Education isn't what some people declare it to be, namely, putting knowledge into souls that lack it, like putting sight into blind eyes. . . . But our present discussion, on the other hand, shows that the power to learn is present in everyone's soul and that the instrument with which each learns is like an eye that cannot be turned from darkness to light without turning the whole body. . . . Then education is the craft concerned with doing this very thing, this turning around, and

31. *Confessions*, III.iv.7, p. 39.

with how the soul can most easily and effectively be made to do it. It isn't the craft for putting sight into the soul. Education takes for granted that sight is there but that it isn't turned the right way or looking where it ought to look and tries to re-direct it appropriately.[32]

Does this notion of turning the soul toward a philosophic idea still have relevance in our contemporary practice of education? Can this idea still move a young person to a life of inquiry and reflection, regardless of their professional path? Can we find in it a way to live with and tame our fallen nature? Should it be a goal of higher education to re-orient the soul of a student toward inquiry into the human good? When we debate the place of liberal education in the university today, these are the questions that we are debating. When we design a college curriculum, and in particular those parts of the curriculum that are required of all students, we implicitly commit ourselves to a view of human nature and to the education that is most appropriate for such a nature. We err fundamentally if we think of education in narrowly instrumental terms—when we confuse it, in other words, with training. To educate means, literally, to "draw out," to *educe* from the student something that is already there and whose successful cultivation represents the fulfillment of the highest human good. Education, in this sense, is liberal education—education not for making a living but for living meaningfully.

Today, the dominant practices of liberal education are a pale shadow of the life-altering program suggested by the classical tradition of learning. Too often, professional practitioners of

---

32. Plato, *Republic*, G.M.A. Grube and C.D.C. Reeve, trans. (Indianapolis and Cambridge: Hackett Publishing Company, 1992), 518, c–e, p. 190.

liberal education—professors and college administrators—have corrupted their activity by subordinating the fundamental goals of education to specialized academic pursuits that only have meaning within their own institutional and career aspirations.

But in a very real sense, a re-orientation of affect and intellect toward goods that are not material, and which constitute the highest conception of human virtue, continues to be the heart of liberal learning. Keeping in view this exalted notion, and the concomitant ongoing investigation of what it is and how to attain it, is a liberal education's way of life.

CHAPTER 2

The Examined Life: Socrates, Plato, and a Little Bit of Aristotle

The first institution resembling a university was founded by Plato on the outskirts of Athens around the year 387 BC. The spot had been named for the mythological hero Academus, so the school came to be known simply as the Academy. Some twenty years after its founding, the Academy received a seventeen-year-old Macedonian student named Aristotle, who remained there until Plato's death in 347 BC and eventually founded his own school of philosophy, the Lyceum. In a move that would come to characterize the philosophical tradition the two men launched, Aristotle made his name not by venerating the doctrines of his teacher, but by disputing them.

These two, Plato and Aristotle, are the uncontested giants of philosophy. I read and loved Plato's dialogues in high school, but did not encounter Aristotle until my freshman year of college. That first encounter didn't go very well. Part of the problem was that the charm and beauty of Plato's writing had set the bar for what I expected of philosophy. Recalling how jarring the contrast can be, I warn my Contemporary Civilization students as they approach Aristotle's *Nicomachean Ethics* (which comes right after Plato's *Republic*) that reading Aristotle can feel like chewing on cardboard. Don't expect enchantment from Aristotle.

The text I read as a freshman was the *Poetics*, and that was also part of the problem. The class was Literature Humanities, the first-year Core Curriculum requirement where, some months after Aristotle, I would read Saint Augustine. Though it wasn't on the official reading list for the course, Professor Wallace Gray dropped the *Poetics* on us in the middle of a spate of ancient Greek plays.

Perhaps I could have gotten past Aristotle's pedantic and arid style, allowing for the fact that the *Poetics* is probably a set of lecture notes rather than a finished work. But beyond the style, I really didn't like what Aristotle had to say. I remember one particular claim that struck me as outrageous: "Beauty is a matter of size and order," he said.[1] Just like that. I couldn't believe the crudity. I didn't just disagree; I found the idea offensive. I could not accept the notion that Beauty is reducible to a formula of constituent elements. To me, it seemed like saying that life is a matter of circulation and respiration. It missed the point. I felt that beauty had to be beyond analysis, irreducible to quantities.

My first paper that semester was a disjointed diatribe against Aristotle for what I took to be his degrading treatment of poetry. Wallace Gray was not impressed. In his comments, he asked that I come see him in his office and wondered why I hadn't appealed to Romantics like Edgar Allan Poe or Friedrich Schlegel, who shared my views on beauty and poetry. I didn't tell him, but the reason I didn't cite them was that I didn't know

---

1. Aristotle, *On Poetry and Style*, translated by G.M.A. Grube (Indianapolis and Cambridge: Hackett Publishing Company, 1989), 1450b, p. 16.

what a Romantic was, or that Poe was one, or who Schlegel was. I also didn't think that it mattered. My views did not derive from literary authorities; they were just what I felt to be true.

So I went to his office in Hamilton Hall to discuss the paper. It was my first use of that college ritual called "the office hour." I felt very distinctly that I was in trouble. I didn't want to go but couldn't find a way to get out of it.

I appeared at the appointed hour and waited on the bench outside his office until the person ahead of me walked out. I went in slowly, frightened. The way I remember it, Professor Gray didn't even say hello but lunged right into the reason he wanted to talk to me: "In your paper," he said, "you come across as rather . . . cocky." That word froze me. It was clear from the way he said it that he expected a response. There was only one way I could respond. I swallowed hard and said timidly: "I'm sorry, Professor, but I don't know what that word means."

This was a poignant instance of an experience I still encounter on occasion: some schoolyard word or expression escaped my book-driven learning of English, and the gap shows up at an inopportune hour. This time, Professor Gray softened his voice and found a nice way of telling me what the word meant. I imagine it was hard to reconcile the voice he encountered in the paper with the shy and mousy student he saw in class. I could see what Professor Gray was getting at, and I knew that what he was interpreting as cockiness was something else, something I could not then name or see through, but which I understood was intertwined with my whole experience at Columbia.

I had arrived at Columbia dazed. My memories of that first year have the jagged vividness of a fever dream. While my English was good enough to be admitted to the College—if barely—my cultural fluency and ability to mingle with fellow students was nowhere close to functional. In some hazy and confused way, I knew this, but couldn't admit it to myself. Professor Gray was detecting my struggle to find a place in a situation I could not decipher.

I took Professor Gray's word—"cocky"—in stride. I didn't feel insulted or deflated. But still, it stung. Professor Gray was poking at the exoskeleton I was building to survive Columbia. That shield created a dead space between me and my classmates that I never bridged as an undergraduate. It would take me many years to see that the distance I kept from my peers was a way of maintaining dignity in the face of an incapacity to engage with them on equal terms. This is what Wallace Gray saw me doing in that paper dismissing Aristotle as insufferably crass, though neither of us knew it.

o o o

Such was my first encounter with Aristotle. With Plato and Socrates, it had been an entirely different story, one with drama, romance, and flair.

It was sophomore year of high school. We had just moved to an apartment on Xenia Street, not far from Fefa's house, where Keysi and I had been living in a basement room. To rent this apartment, we pooled together money from Keysi's job as a security guard (he was also attending Queens College by now) and $300 I had saved from a summer job in the mail room of LaGuardia Community College. The rest of the money for the first month's rent and one month's security deposit came from Elías, an acquaintance from Cambita who had been living in a rented room nearby. Elías had gotten a job as a mailman, and this allowed him to upgrade his living situation and prepare for the arrival from DR of his wife, who would eventually live with us as well.

We moved into the three-bedroom apartment on January 16, 1989. Elías had the master bedroom, Mom and Ray the one next to it, and Keysi the tiny one by the living room. I'd sleep with Mom and Ray, in a small bed next to the one they shared. This may sound tight for a teenager, but it was much better than living in someone else's basement, not having your own bed, and only seeing your mother every couple of weeks.

Next door to us lived a friendly elderly couple who didn't speak Spanish and with whom, therefore, we hardly had any interaction. One evening that winter, on a garbage night, those cordial Americans rid themselves of a big pile of books, putting them out on the curb for the sanitation truck to pick up early the next morning. I saw the stack of books and immediately went to inspect it. Some of the books were gorgeous, with hard covers and gold-edged pages like the expensive Bibles ministers and very pious people carried. I wanted to take them all, but there were too many, and we had no bookshelves. Besides, my English wasn't good enough to get through any grown-up book without great difficulty. In the end, I grabbed only two hardbacks. One of them was a volume of Plato's dialogues.

This was one of the many weirdnesses of Americans: they threw away perfectly good stuff. It was the common practice of the growing Dominican population of Queens to scour the twice-weekly piles of trash on the sidewalks, looking for treasure. And treasure there was—couches, dressers, chairs, TVs, lamps, and other valuable items in perfectly good condition or needing only minor repairs. These findings would be the stuff of legend back in DR. People's imagination was gripped by the idea of a place of such affluence that you could make a living by simply picking up discarded items off the street.

Whenever someone arrived from Nueba Yol—which was what we called the United States—the first hours were always a feverish marathon of astonishing tales about life in the US. These stories would produce laughter, tears, and general amazement. Fueled by continuous rounds of coffee served in tiny cups, the newly arrived would dispense wisdom, distribute presents, and deliver parcels sent by friends and family in New York. They would radiate a kind of luminescence, like they had just stepped out of a *telenovela*. Everything out of the suitcase would be suffused with the aroma of Nueba Yol, a peculiar smell of prosperous cleanliness that clung to clothes and lingered in the suitcases for days. Kids, myself among them, would stand on the side, wild-eyed, hoping some exotic treat would emerge from a purse or a pocket, as it often did.

So there I stood before a trove of precious books. Someone had thrown them away. They were beautiful even as mere objects. In ways I could not have understood, before me was the treasure I had come to America to find. I didn't know how to choose, and it was too cold to stand there looking through them. The two books I eventually took were among the most beautiful of the pile, from a collection called the Harvard Classics— ostentatious volumes designed much less to be read than to adorn stately book shelves in wealthy people's homes. The two tomes I took, and which I still own, were the second and forty-sixth volumes of the series: *Plato, Epictetus, Marcus Aurelius* and *Elizabethan Drama I.* I took the plays because I recognized one of the two gold-letter names on the spine: *Marlowe, Shakespeare.* The name Plato was also familiar; Epictetus and Marcus Aurelius I had never heard of, but they sounded classical enough.

○ ○ ○

The Harvard Classics series was published in 1910 and is sometimes called "the President's Five-Foot Shelf." The "President" was the then retiring President of Harvard University, Charles W. Eliot, who apparently had said in a speech to working-class men (who could have never aspired to attend Harvard College) that they could get the rudiments of a liberal education by reading for fifteen minutes every day "with devotion," from a set of books that could fit in a five-foot shelf. When invited by the enterprising publisher Peter Collier to name the books, Eliot came up with the fifty-one volumes that make up the Harvard Universal Classics collection.[2]

The impulse to compile a list of essential works—"the furniture of the mind" of an educated person, as the Yale Report of 1828 put it—is understandable and has a pedigree as old as literature itself. But every list is a standing invitation to criticism for what it leaves out and what it chooses to include. The lists never age well.

In contemporary academic debate, where critiques of the canon almost always come wagging the finger of social justice, President Eliot's list would draw fire for not containing any women, but he might well get a pass for skipping Aristotle. The salient failings of the list would be ethical rather than intellectual—not that these two are always clearly separable. Today's academic criticism bends toward moral reprimand: it doesn't just illuminate, it burns; it doesn't just judge, it condemns; it doesn't just reject, it cancels. This is a primary reason academics—and I mean primarily those of us in the humanities and the humanistic social sciences—are so reluctant to present value judgments in their scholarly work. To put it more accurately, we are reluctant to reveal the values we hold and which unavoidably inform our research. Every position that can be

---

2. See Adam Kirsch, "The 'Five-foot Shelf' Reconsidered," *Harvard Magazine* (Nov.–Dec. 2001).

pinned down—like any list of "essential works"—can be at-
tacked, and as with President Eliot's list, some attacks will seek
to expose your value judgments as morally corrupt or complicit
in larger systems of exclusion and exploitation. As a sort of in-
oculation against the career-ending peril of being unmasked as
a moral retrograde, a good contemporary scholar will invent
ways of saying many things and performing spectacular feats of
erudition without assuming any clear position on matters of
consequence.

In designing college curricula, there is a corresponding re-
luctance to prescribe any specific content. This is most evident
where it matters most: in programs in general education. American colleges, harkening to a liberal arts tradition, still tend to
prescribe a significant amount of coursework that lies outside
the student's major or specialization. These general education
requirements are meant to ensure that, in addition to professional or pre-professional training, all students receive a common and non-specialized—that is, a liberal—education. General education requirements emphasize the humanities as well
as basic skills like scientific literacy and effective writing. But
rather than specifying any definite content for these classes, colleges have typically required that students sample a range of
disciplinary approaches outside of their major and have called
this general education. The tendency is to focus on competencies rather than on knowledge and on ways of knowing rather
than on things to be known.

I have heard college deans and presidents extoll the merits
of low-requirement curricula and of student choice in designing
their own courses of study. Why not let students pick for themselves what they find most relevant or appealing (or easiest to
earn an "A" in)? Some schools even boast of having no requirements at all apart from completing a certain number of credits.

What better way of responding to—or dodging—the fervent calls for diversity and representation in curricula than to define no curriculum at all?

Yet the underlying force driving the disintegration of undergraduate curricula is not a passion for student choice or a commitment to diversity, but a crisis of consensus among academic humanists about what things are most worth *knowing*. And because debates about curricula are likely to be had in moral terms—not between what is educationally good or bad but between what is ethically pure or corrupt—it is simply easier for colleges to avoid having them altogether. Thus colleges have largely withdrawn from their traditional responsibility of offering students a considered view of just what aspects of our intellectual and cultural heritage are most worth their attention.

The claim that in today's America there is no sufficiently shared intellectual and cultural heritage to justify common study is disproven by the fact that public life is transacted through a range of shared institutions, norms, categories, and values in which we all participate and in which we all have a stake. These institutions, norms, categories, and values have a history that, though riddled with debate, constitutes our shared heritage. My being a brown immigrant from the Dominican Republic does not make the Constitution less relevant to me than it is to my wife, a white woman born in rural Michigan. She is no closer to and no further from Homer and Socrates than I am or than our two-year-old son will grow up to be. For this reason, what is often identified as the Western tradition has a special claim in general education curricula in societies that have emerged from or have been strongly influenced by that tradition.

o o o

Presenting—if always provisionally—a common body of provocations, debates, and questions as deserving the attention of every undergraduate at a given institution is a basic responsibility of a college faculty. In the case of the humanities, this will probably mean a specific list of texts or issues. In a way, this is what President Eliot's Five-Foot Shelf tried to do.

It proved a good little piece of business, selling over 3,500 sets (of fifty-one volumes each) in the first twenty years of publication. That's a lot of hardcover books. I wonder how many of them ended up in attics, in dead libraries, and in piles like the one from my next-door neighbors in Corona, Queens, circa 1989. How many of them ended up in the hands of someone who could not have aspired to go to Harvard but who read them with devotion and gleaned from them the rudiments of a liberal education? At least two of the volumes did. Or, to be perfectly accurate, one, and in that volume, only the three dialogues of Plato, which I began to read immediately after picking up the books.

That initial reading of Plato did a lot of things for me. One of them was to catalyze a friendship with a person who would become a lifelong mentor: John Philippides. I had first met Mr. Philippides while in the eighth grade, when Keysi took me to John Bowne High School, the public school where he was a junior and where I would join him as a freshman the following year. Mr. Philippides says he remembers my diminutive figure peering at him shyly from behind my brother's legs.

I had no idea then, and for a long time, what a remarkable place John Bowne High School was. School officials boasted that Bowne was the most ethnically diverse high school in New York City, with fifty-one different languages spoken by its students. But that didn't mean much to me, since Queens was the only part of New York I knew, and Bowne was simply like Queens.

Like many large New York City public schools, Bowne was, in fact, many schools at once, with students inhabiting starkly different academic and social tracks. I was in the track of academic achievers, which, in a school full of immigrants, was a high-achieving track indeed. I was far from the best student in that cohort, but finding myself in that school-within-a-school may be put down as one of the great fortunes of my life. This group had some native-born Americans, but most of us were immigrants with various degrees of English proficiency. It was a sort of cloister made up of students who assumed that, when homework was assigned, one had to do it; that when a test was announced, one had to study for it; that when a teacher said something, one had to pay attention; and that each teacher, no matter how odd or witless, was owed a degree of respectful deference. That cloister nurtured and protected me from what otherwise felt like a chaotic throng of wild adolescents. I was always the smallest and skinniest kid in class, and my default mode at school was to be terrified. I would arrive at school early and linger late to avoid the crowd; I would sign up for "service periods" rather than eat lunch in the cafeteria; I would seek out friends among the teachers and security guards rather than among my peers.

I had gotten to school early one day that sophomore year of high school, Plato in hand, for a "research" biology class. This before-school class was offered by Dr. Martin Allen, the biology department chair, who hoped some projects would emerge from it for the annual science fair. The project I had chosen was "The effect of aspirin on eye-color crosses of *drosophila melanogaster*." Most days, there was little to do on the project, but I was happy to get to school early, have a warm breakfast in a near empty cafeteria, and go tend to my fruit flies.

On one of these quiet mornings, I was sitting in the hallway perusing my volume of Plato when Mr. Philippides walked by.

The glistening pages of the book must have caught his eye, and he approached to ask what I was reading. I told him, and he was delighted. I could see the teacher-fire in his owl eyes light up. He seemed to know a lot about Plato and Socrates, and was clearly dying to tell me about it. He joked about them being his relatives, he being Greek and all. He encouraged me to tell him what I thought of what I was reading.

Later that day, during the homeroom mini-period, I stopped by Mr. Philippides's classroom. I had a vocabulary question. I wanted to know what the word "gadfly" meant. More fire in his eyes. He described something that sounded to me like a leech with wings, and he asked me to find him after school so we could talk more. I did, and that began a string of many, many hours, over the next several years, of extended after-school conversations about All Topics of Learning. The majority of these conversations went entirely over my head. But I absorbed all I could of the dense intellectual disquisitions; above all, I delighted in the shower of learned attention and interest Mr. Philippides poured on me. When it came time to apply to college, it was Mr. Philippides who encouraged me to apply to Columbia, and he was the only person to whom I showed my personal statement. And that senior year, as if guided by prophetic insight, he gave me the new Robert Fagles translation of the *Iliad* for Christmas.

It is a strange stroke of fortune that Socrates should be the figure to arise from that pile of books on the sidewalk, like a genie rubbed out of a lamp. There's probably no more accessible, compelling, and seminal point of entry to liberal education than Plato's Socrates. He is the archetypal teacher, the archetypal free-thinker, the archetypal intellectual saint. Alfred North Whitehead famously said that "the safest general characterization of the European philosophical tradition is that it consists of a series of footnotes to Plato."[3] But no, it is rather a series of footnotes to Socrates. I could not have found a better place from which to start my education in great books, and no better guide than the man who had been a Greek immigrant boy on a Pennsylvania farm and had made his way to Princeton. He had retired from a real-estate business to become a New York City public school teacher and, with luck, save a few souls—his own included.

o o o

The Socrates I rescued from a pile of trash is full of romance. How could my hungry teenage heart resist him? The three dialogues in the book span the period from his trial to his execution: The *Apology*, the *Crito*, and the *Phaedo*. The *Apology* records Socrates's defense of himself before an Athenian jury. He was brought to court, at age seventy, accused of corrupting the young and of introducing new gods to the city. He was found guilty and sentenced to death.

The next dialogue, the *Crito*, flows from the absurdity of the trial. Things got out of hand. No one could have possibly really wanted such an outcome. It would be ridiculous for Athens to put to death a seventy-year-old-man for engaging in the activity—annoying as it might be—that Socrates was engaged in. Socrates's old and wealthy friend, Crito, visits him in prison, having made arrangements for his escape. Athenian authorities seem embarrassed by what's happening and are ready to turn a blind eye if his friends were to arrange for Socrates to leave Athens. So Crito is there, with only a few days to go before the

---

3. Alfred North Whitehead, *Process and Reality, Corrected Edition*, David Ray Griffin and Donald W. Sherburne, eds. (New York: Free Press, 1978), p. 39.

execution, ready to whisk Socrates away. But Socrates says, "No, I can't go." Then he argues that to run away would be to betray everything he has lived for and that his entire way of life demands that he accept the death sentence imposed lawfully by the city. It is a devastating argument that leaves Crito completely defeated. His last words in the dialogue are "I have nothing to say, Socrates."

The *Phaedo*, the last dialogue in the collection, purports to be a record of Socrates's last conversation, in which he argues, and claims to demonstrate, the immortality of the soul. The dialogue then ends with a heart-wrenching description of Socrates "calmly and easily" drinking the poison, lying down, and quietly dying: "Such was the end of our comrade," says Phaedo, "a man who, we would say, was of all we have known the best, and also the wisest and the most upright."[4]

o o o

Socrates's defense is simple and plain. It paints a quintessential picture of a life devoted to the pursuit of truth and virtue— what he conceives as the philosophic life. His words to the jury come in three speeches. In the first, and longest, he defends himself against the charges brought against him. He fails at this, and the jury finds him guilty as charged. According to Athenian practice, after a guilty verdict, the jury would choose between a punishment proposed by the accuser and one proposed by

---

4. Instead of the old Benjamin Jowett translation in the Harvard Classics edition, throughout this book I use a contemporary translation: Plato, *The Trial and Death of Socrates*, trans. by G.M.A Grube, rev. by John M. Cooper, 3rd ed. (Indianapolis and Cambridge: Hackett Publishing Company, 2000). This brief quotation is from 118a, p. 67.

the accused. Socrates's accusers propose death. The second speech of the *Apology* is Socrates's counterproposal. Initially, he suggests that he be given free meals at the city's expense, but then, at the urging of Plato and other rich friends, he agrees to a fine which they will pay for him, since he himself has no money. According to the ancient biographer Diogenes Laertius, the margin of the vote to condemn Socrates to death was larger than the one that found him guilty. His second speech, in other words, was an even bigger failure than his first. The third speech in the *Apology* records Socrates's admonition to the jury after its decision to have him executed.

Socrates's initial defense speech doesn't dazzle. At least, it didn't dazzle me. It didn't have the magnanimity and passion I expected from a man in his situation. I remember thinking it was sort of half-hearted; I wanted a heroic blast, a discharge of thunder. But at times, especially early on in the speech, Socrates seems whiny and a little conceited, complaining about popular depictions of him like the one in Aristophanes's play *The Clouds*, where he is viciously and hilariously mocked. His defense sometimes seems calculated precisely to turn off the jury. Such is the moment when he claims to be a "gadfly":

> Indeed, men of Athens, I am far from making a defense now on my own behalf, as might be thought, but on yours, to prevent you from wrongdoing by mistreating the god's gift to you by condemning me; for if you kill me you will not easily find another like me. I was attached to this city by the god—though it seems a ridiculous thing to say—as upon a great and noble horse which was somewhat sluggish because of its size and needed to be stirred up by a kind of gadfly. It is to fulfill some such function that I believe the god has placed me in the city. I never cease to rouse each and every

one of you, to persuade and reproach you all day long and everywhere I find myself in your company.[5]

Really? Doesn't Socrates see that this line of defense isn't going to help? That he sounds arrogant and presumptuous? It's as if Socrates has in view not the jury in front of him, but the intellectual tradition he would launch. It's as if he is looking past his fellow citizens to a lineage of dissident intellectuals and telling them, "Your business is to irritate authorities, to challenge the status quo, to ask embarrassing and obnoxious questions of those who claim a public mandate, and to be prepared to pay the ultimate cost for doing so." Compelling as this may sound now, it could not have landed well on the audience of the moment. Nor could it have been helpful to talk about a "divine sign," a "voice" that since childhood had spoken to him ordering him to abstain from doing certain things like entering politics.[6]

Despite his questionable rhetorical choices, the overall impact of Socrates's self-defense is powerful. Its force comes upon you gradually, evenly, and you might not even notice it until it's too late to resist.

He tells the story of an oracle of the god at Delphi declaring that no one was wiser than Socrates.[7] He could not believe this at first, he tells the jury, and his whole philosophical quest became an effort to understand what that oracle could have possibly meant. In that investigation, he approached anyone he could find with a reputation for wisdom and systematically questioned him (it was always a man, of course)[8] about subjects

---

5. *Trial and Death*, 30d–e.

6. *Trial and Death*, 31d.

7. *Trial and Death*, 21a.

8. Curiously, in the *Symposium*, Socrates claims to have been the student of a mysterious woman named Diotima from whom he learned everything he knew

such as the meaning of piety, virtue, justice, and the nature of the human good. Beginning with politicians, and then turning to poets and ending with craftsmen, Socrates found that "those with the highest reputation were the most deficient,"[9] so that ignorance was distributed in the Athenian population in inverse proportion to the reputation for wisdom. The early Platonic dialogues offer account after account of such cringing encounters between Socrates and his often exasperated interlocutors. "The wise" prove not to be wise at all and, in fact, emerge as all the more ignorant because of their conceit of wisdom. They were the most ignorant of their own ignorance. After these interviews, Socrates would walk away thinking, "I am wiser than this man; it is likely that neither of us knows anything worthwhile, but he thinks he knows something when he does not, whereas when I do not know, neither do I think I know; so I am likely to be wiser to this small extent, that I do not think I know what I do not know."[10] But this hard-won insight has come at the expense of becoming a pest to the leading men of Athens, some of whom were surely among the jurors who voted in favor of ridding the city of this loafer.

Socrates captivated me. His method of conversation and inquiry suggested a way of life I wanted to live. I have seen Socrates have this same effect on other young people. Every summer for over a decade, I have taught these dialogues to rising high school seniors through a program at Columbia called Freedom and Citizenship. The program is a collaboration between the Center for American Studies and the Double Discovery Center,

---

about love. We know nothing of this woman except what Socrates says there, so the account is probably made up.

9. *Trial and Death*, 22a.

10. *Trial and Death*, 21d.

a community outreach organization that works with low-income students in New York City. Freedom and Citizenship begins with a residential experience at Columbia built around a three-week seminar in which students spend one week reading ancient texts—Plato, Aristotle, Thucydides; another week reading texts from the enlightenment—Hobbes, Locke, Rousseau, Jefferson; and a third week looking at America—Abraham Lincoln, Frederick Douglass, Martin Luther King Jr., etc. All of the students in the class come from low-income households and hope to be first in their families to attend college. After the summer, over the course of the students' senior year of high school, they are paired with a Columbia undergraduate who serves as a college-application mentor. Throughout their senior year, they also come to campus every other week to work on a civic-engagement project in which they pursue concerns that emerged during discussions in the summer seminar. The program is free. More 300 students have now participated, and nearly 100 percent of them have enrolled in college, with many of them continuing on to graduate school.

Every year in this program, I see students undergo a kind of inner awakening. Many of them react to Socrates in the same way I did: they take his words seriously and personally. One student that sticks out in my mind had come to us after several years living in foster care, having been removed by child-welfare authorities from an abusive mother in Harlem. At the end of the program, she spoke movingly about how she saw herself in Socrates, how he spoke to her deepest sense of who she was. A few years later, she graduated from a liberal arts college, and I went to her graduation party. It's hard to describe the intensity of feeling that pervaded the occasion. She had majored in philosophy and had won various prizes at graduation, one of which explicitly compared her to Socrates. She was going to spend the next year in South America, learning Spanish. Something about her encounter with Socrates had stuck deeply and will probably continue to influence the shape of her life.

When I discuss the *Apology* with high school students in the summer class, I draw their attention to Socrates's statement that he has been ordered by the god "to live the life of a philosopher, to examine myself and others."[11] For Socrates this, simply this, is the philosophic life: to examine yourself and others. What could that mean, to examine yourself? Are you not fully known to yourself? Are you not transparent to yourself? What could you possibly learn from yourself that you don't already know? Somehow, this inward turn is primary for Socrates. Next comes the investigation of others. Perhaps after that, we can get to other things to be known and investigated. Your own mind and that of others is ground zero for the philosophic life. And this process of self-investigation is not only reflective, but conversational—there are things about yourself that you can only see through conversation with others.

More than a thousand years after Socrates, Montaigne would take this approach to heart and produce one of the greatest meditations on the human condition ever written: the series of sketches by which he invented the genre of the essay, and which he published under that very name, *Essays*. There, he calls Socrates "our master" and notes: "I study myself more than any other subject. This is my metaphysics, this is my physics."[12] This orientation toward honest self-examination constitutes the most demanding of tasks and also the most important. A teacher in the humanities can give students no greater gift than the

---

11. *Trial and Death*, 28e.

12. Michele de Montaigne, *Essays*, J. M. Cohen, trans. (London: Penguin Classics, 1958), pp. 403, 353.

revelation of the self as a primary object of lifelong investigation, the habit of seeing their ordinary human experience with critical self-awareness. This is the basic task of a liberal education—not to deliver truths, but to cultivate the life-altering disposition to look inward even as one looks outward.

This dual orientation is also the key to understanding great literature. If you want to understand Shakespeare's *Macbeth*, scholarly articles and summaries can only take you so far. To understand *Macbeth* deeply, you have look into yourself deeply. What is it like to be gripped by the lust for power? What is the taste of glory? What is the shock of betrayal? What is the psychic havoc of unassuageable guilt? Literature can be humanizing precisely for this capacity to shine a light on aspects of one's inner life that might otherwise go unexplored or be seen only superficially. It demands the most difficult and most decisive of psychic tasks: to look unflinchingly at yourself.

According to Socrates, the philosophical life is inseparable from this activity of self-scrutiny and involves open-ended and in-depth conversations with others. And this isn't just an activity for professional philosophers but the most important endeavor in any human life. In one of the most forceful moments in his speech, he drives the point home, addressing the jury directly:

If you said to me in this regard: "Socrates, we do not believe Anytus now; we acquit you, but only on condition that you spend no more time on this investigation and do not practice philosophy, and if you are caught doing so you will die"; if, as I say, you were to acquit me on those terms, I would say to you: "Men of Athens, I am grateful and I am your friend, but I will obey the god rather than you, and as long as I draw breath and am able, I shall not cease to practice philosophy, to exhort you and in my usual way to point out to anyone of you whom I happen to meet: "Good Sir, you are an Athenian, a citizen of the greatest city with the greatest reputation for both wisdom and power; are you not ashamed of your eagerness to possess as much wealth, reputation and honors as possible, while you do not care for nor give thought to wisdom or truth, or the best possible state of your soul?" Then, if one of you disputes this and says he does care, I shall not let him go at once or leave him, but I shall question him, examine him and test him, and if I do not think he has attained the goodness that he says he has, I shall reproach him because he attaches little importance to the most important things and greater importance to inferior things. I shall treat in this way anyone I happen to meet, young and old, citizen and stranger, and more so the citizens because you are more kindred to me. Be sure that this is what the god orders me to do, and I think there is no greater blessing for the city than my service to the god. For I go around doing nothing but persuading both young and old among you not to care for your body or your wealth in preference to or as strongly as for the best possible state of your soul, as I say to you: "Wealth does not bring about excellence, but excellence makes wealth and everything else good for men, both individually and collectively."[13]

I do not recall exactly what impact these words had on me when I first read them, but today they affect me powerfully. They feel more relevant and more urgent in the 2020s than they did in the 1980s; indeed, they strike me as more acutely applicable in our twenty-first-century society than in Socrates's

---

13. *Trial and Death*, 29d–30b.

fifth-century Athens. They speak compellingly to the young people who show up in my classrooms. Although students come to college looking to secure their economic future, most of them also arrive with hushed but persistent doubts about the prevailing value system of our market-driven culture.

At Columbia, students are conscious of being in the top echelon of a vicious ladder of competition and prestige, but many of them seem to be grappling with the realization that such achievements don't satisfy their longing for meaning. Rather than the entitled and fragile "snowflakes" some observers have described, I find my classrooms populated with young people of real depth and earnestness who, like me at their age, are racked with existential anxiety and are struggling with the threat of meaninglessness. They are obsessed with moral questions and wonder whether the frantic pursuit of success, wealth, and status will actually satisfy their deepest thirst. Socrates's words speak directly to students who go to college looking for a way to ground not just their careers, but their lives.

In my experience, professors are reluctant to "go there" with their students and with themselves. Yet these Socratic questions are the lifeblood of the humanist profession—that is, of the humanist calling and vocation. The academic humanities are bound to be feeble and anemic, inauthentic and ham-fisted, unless they take these questions seriously and place them at the center of their practice. These are not questions for academic journals, but questions that professors need to ask of students, of colleagues, and of themselves. Liberal arts teaching and scholarship must emerge organically from their whole lives, not just from their career paths. I cannot see but that a series of high-minded personal commitments are prerequisite for the authentic exercise of the humanist profession. It is such personal commitments that animate Socrates in his philosophical activity and that provide the steel in his spine as he addresses the Athenian jury.

As the *Apology* proceeds through the three set speeches, the drama builds, the stakes get higher and higher, and the trial tumbles absurdly and tragically into disaster. We come to the close of Socrates's speeches with a picture of the archetypal philosopher—disdainful of riches and power, convinced of his own ignorance but skeptical of those who claim to possess knowledge, unswerving in his pursuit of truth, an irritant to authorities, a magnet to the young. "The most important thing," he says to Crito in his prison cell shortly before execution, "is not life, but the good life."[14] For Socrates, a life worth living can only be sustained by values worth dying for.

o o o

It did not escape me, when I read Plato in the heat of Christian fervor, that the outlines of Socrates's story were also the outlines of the story of Jesus. Nor did I fail to note that this story had been written hundreds of years before Jesus's birth and that, contrary to the preaching I was hearing, Jesus had not cornered the market on virtue. These realizations were an intimation that there were more things in heaven and earth than were dreamt of in the evangelical Christianity I was adopting.

But there was another figure Socrates reminded me of even more pointedly: my own father. Their reputations were not dissimilar. Except for the brief period when he worked in a government agricultural research center (it's not clear to me what it was he did there), Dad never held a regular job. When I was very small—I barely remember this—he was a tailor and had

---

14. *Trial and Death*, 48b.

converted part of the bedroom into his shop, with a door to the outside. He had taught himself how to make clothes for people and started making a living from it while still a bachelor. By the time I was growing up, he had stopped making clothes for people and made them for furniture instead, picking up odd jobs as a reupholsterer. He provided for the family, but barely. He did not bring home the income he could have brought if he had applied himself to making money, which everybody wanted him to do. The easiest way would have been to accept a job from one of the many politicians who were trying to silence him. But, no, Dad would not compromise the privilege of castigating public authorities, inveighing against government corruption, and denouncing *el imperialismo yanqui.* Making money was always done under the compulsion of pressing need. He seemed to feel that material prosperity was beneath him, to the acute dismay of those who depended on him. But, somehow, I accepted this without resentment. It was his genius to raise me poor but without my knowing it, or to the extent that I knew it, considering it a mark of virtue rather than a badge of inferiority.

During the day, if Dad was working at his sewing machine or cutting table, he would usually be surrounded by a coterie of people, mainly drifting young men and town irregulars (Cambita's many "crazies" were always well-represented), debating some political, historical, or metaphysical question. In the evenings, the conversation moved to the front porch, the *galería,* where a rotating cast of locals would vie for a seat in one of the continuously mended rocking chairs. Here, every curious piece of knowledge or strange fact and happening in Cambita or the world would become the subject of earnest discussion. These almost nightly symposia involved regular attendees as well as passersby in one of the busiest of Cambita's few streets. Some people called it *la escuelita*—the little school. The spontaneous and freewheeling sessions in the *galería* were a vivid example of the "free and daring speculation on the highest subjects" that John Stuart Mill recommended in *On Liberty*.[15] No god ever declared him the wisest man in Cambita, but if a god had been pressed on the point, I do not doubt he would have come out with the name Roosevelt Montás Sr., known to all by his nickname, Malliguín.

o o o

Socrates's *Apology* is, fundamentally, a justification for the philosophic life. "The unexamined life," he tells his audience of Athenian citizens after he has been found guilty, "is not worth living."[16] By the time I was reading this in high school, my English was good enough to understand clearly what Socrates was saying. These words were not just about something that had happened a long time ago to an old man in Greece. They had meaning for me right where I was and just as I was. What I was gleaning from the text was not about Ancient Greece or about philosophy, but about how I was to live my life. I was reading Socrates in the same way that I was reading the Bible. Even though they did not carry the divine authority I had accepted in Scripture, Socrates's words offered an invitation to a certain mode of life. They confirmed in me what had been an unarticulated but distinct sense of the kind of life most worth living. Something I had lost sight of in the confusion of losing an entire world when I left Cambita was gleaming at me from the pages of this old book I had found.

---

15. John Stuart Mill, *On Liberty and Other Essays*, John Gray, ed., Oxford World Classics (Oxford: Oxford University Press, 1991, 1998), p. 38.

16. *Trial and Death*, 38a.

∘ ∘ ∘

The heroism of Socrates is most evident in the *Crito*, a short dialogue that takes place in Socrates's jail cell a few days before his death. Socrates has been in prison for a month awaiting execution, which cannot happen until a certain ship returns from a religious mission it has been conducting on behalf of Athens. The ship has arrived at a nearby port, only a day's journey away. The fateful day is at hand. A plan has been hatched for his escape, the guard has been bribed, and Socrates's childhood friend Crito—who, like him, has reached an improbable old age and, unlike him, has become a wealthy landowner—comes to persuade Socrates to flee.

The dialogue opens with a tender scene in which Socrates wakes up early in the morning to find Crito sitting in his cell.

SOCRATES: Why have you come so early, Crito? Or is it not still early?

CRITO: It certainly is.

SOCRATES: How early?

CRITO: Early dawn.

SOCRATES: I am surprised that the warder was willing to listen to you.

CRITO: He is quite friendly by now, Socrates. I have been here often and I have given him something.

SOCRATES: Have you just come, or have you been here for some time?

CRITO: A fair time.

SOCRATES: Then why did you not wake me right away but sit there in silence?

CRITO: By Zeus, no, Socrates. I would not myself want to be in distress and awake so long. I have been surprised to see you so peacefully asleep. It was on purpose that I did not wake you, so that you should spend your time most agreeably. Often in the past throughout my life, I have considered the way you live happy, and especially so now that you bear your present misfortune so easily and lightly.

SOCRATES: It would not be fitting at my age to resent the fact that I must die now.[17]

The old man Crito arrives while it's still dark and finds his childhood pal peacefully asleep. Rather than wake him, he sits there in silence, looking at him. The tenderness of this scene, captured as much by the staging as by what is said, is an example of why Plato, in addition to being a great philosopher, is a superb dramatist. Crito sits there as the rising light of dawn begins to illuminate Socrates's face and bring his peculiar features into relief. Crito recollects their long life in the tumult of fifth-century Athens, with its wars, regime changes, and stupendous outburst of arts and letters. He thinks about how Socrates has lived his life and reflects on his feeling that, somehow, Socrates, though penniless and now in big trouble, has probably lived the happiest life of the two. Even now, awaiting death, Socrates sleeps soundly and seems undisturbed by his predicament. Xenophon tells us that in his old age, Socrates began to take dance lessons, and we know from the *Phaedo* that during his month in jail he took to writing poetry. Perhaps Crito was thinking about Socrates dancing and writing poetry. Or perhaps he was thinking about the loneliness of his own old age, made more acute by the loss of this dear friend.

---

17. *Trial and Death*, 43b.

Socrates tells Crito that he has just had a dream in which a beautiful woman dressed in white approached him and said, "Socrates, may you arrive at fertile Phthia on the third day,"[18] quoting what Achilles says about himself in Book 9 of Homer's *Iliad*. Socrates thinks this is a prophetic dream signaling that the ship will not arrive on that day, as Crito expects, but on the day after, with the execution the day after that, "on the third day." Regardless, Crito launches his bid to persuade Socrates to escape right then and there—perhaps to Crito's friends in Thessaly, who would welcome and cherish him. Crito deploys a whole battery of arguments that Socrates, in his usual question-and-answer style, demolishes one by one. One of Crito's arguments rang a particular bell in my own life:

> Moreover, I think you are betraying your sons by going away and leaving them, when you could bring them up and educate them. You thus show no concern for what their fate may be. They will probably have the usual fate of orphans. Either one should not have children, or one should share with them to the end the toil of upbringing and education. You seem to me to choose the easiest path, whereas one should choose the path a good and courageous man would choose, particularly when one claims throughout one's life to care for virtue.[19]

Ouch. That last line was a little bit below the belt. But even without the zinger, the argument carries force not just as it concerns Socrates's current predicament, but as it concerns his whole way of life, with its voluntary poverty. Socrates might choose that life for himself, but is it right for him to choose a life of poverty for his children?

---

18. *Trial and Death*, 44b.
19. *Trial and Death*, 45c–d.

When I first read Crito's argument, and all the way down to this day, this passage raises uncomfortable questions for me. As various family members were eager to point out (always, it seemed to me, with a tinge of Schadenfreude), my father, who came to the US along with my brother and me in 1985 and could have stayed, decided not to. He walked away, leaving us in the charge of our ill-equipped mother, penniless, and in the frightening New York City of the 1980s.

Dad could not endure the humiliating marginality and helplessness of what would be his life in Nueba Yol. He went back to Cambita. Broken-hearted and with a cloud of opprobrium hanging over his head, he left. He had no phone in Cambita and there was no mail service by which to maintain regular communication, so his departure meant that his presence in my life would be reduced to the rare letter and the even rarer visit, both of which would entirely stop after he lost his visa. We had come to the country on green cards, so he could not stay out of the US longer than six months, and he could not afford to buy a plane ticket every six months just to keep his visa valid. After exhausting his eligibility for a special two-year permit, he let his green card expire. A green card, let be it noted, is the most coveted visa a foreigner can get, granting permanent residence in the United States and automatic eligibility to apply for citizenship. It is a thing for which Dominicans literally kill themselves, braving waves in wooden boats to land on US soil in Puerto Rico. He let it expire, along with the possibility of entering the country where his teenage sons were trying to find a way to live. This is how it came to pass that our father abandoned us.

Nobody approved.

I have not been able to muster any real resentment toward Dad for this. I've tried, but the results have always been half-hearted. My wife suggests that this is partly in self-defense, allowing me to preserve a certain image of him that is important to my own sense of self. Perhaps. I remember his misery the few times he attempted to establish himself in the US. It was oppressive to me. Had he stayed, I think it would have poisoned my life.

In his response to Crito, Socrates hardly engages this argument, offering a passing dismissal: "As for those questions you raise about money, reputation, the upbringing of children, Crito, these considerations in truth belong to those people who easily put men to death and would bring them to life again if they could, without thinking."[20] Socrates's deflection did not apply in my case.

How do I evaluate whether my father made the right decision? Things have worked out alright for me, my older brother, and Mom. And they have worked out alright for his DR family, including my two half-siblings. Our relationship is fine. But how do I judge whether he did as he should have done? How do I measure his responsibility to me and my brother against his responsibility to my younger siblings in DR and to his partner there, who was for a time my stepmother? These questions, which I asked myself and continue to ask myself, are also the questions my father had to ask of himself, and answer. I never have to spend much time with him before realizing, again, that this decision left a wound in him that has never healed. I see this in his solicitude and deference to me; I see it in the joy that overwhelms him when he first sees me after a period of absence; I see it in the tears that predictably flood his eyes every time we say goodbye.

Like the questions that mattered to Socrates—about the nature of the good, justice, truth, and the life worth living—my

---

20. *Trial and Death*, 48c.

questions are not subject to a final determination; they are ir-reducible to calculable certitude. Yet they are the proper subject of rational inquiry, as Socrates insists.

A liberal education is one that takes the complicated condition of human freedom seriously and addresses itself to its dilemmas and to the urgency of its lived experience. To think and reason through these kinds of questions is to learn to live with them in an honest and ongoing way. These questions from a decisive period in my development, and about a formative relationship for my sense of self, shape the character of my inner life; they are questions in whose tensions I improvise my daily existence, including the writing of this book. While the specific details of the questions will vary from individual to individual, every human life is like this, balanced between imponderables. The great questions of philosophy and the unique questions that concern only me, in my individual particularity, are always intersecting, always infiltrating each other. Learning to see my particular in the universal is no small help in living sanely.

Was my receptiveness to Socrates and to his uncompromising vision of the philosophic life a way to idealize my father's abandonment, a way to assimilate into my personality an event that threatened to de-stabilize its foundations? It must be at least partly this. Yet I am not the only one who has been roused to a new sense of wakefulness by Socrates's vision of the life most worth living. My individual psychology does not exhaust its meaning, but its meaning illuminates and, at the same time, helps shape my individual psychology. I would place a text that can do this for a large variety of individuals and over many generations in my five-foot shelf of essential books and in my ideal general education curriculum. Liberal exploration of such texts in a classroom inevitably involves reflection on the deepest levels of one's sense of self.

Socrates keeps bringing Crito back to the meaning of a life well-lived. He refutes his various arguments and introduces an understanding of the relation of a free citizen to the state that has been enormously influential in the history of political thought and which is still fertile ground for debate. Socrates argues that he is bound to obey the laws of Athens, even in this case, when the laws have decreed his death. He says that by choosing to live in the city, fully cognizant of its laws and how they were administered, he had tacitly consented to abide by them. The fact that he is now personally harmed by the application of laws under which he has consented to live does not invalidate his obligation to submit to them.

With this argument, Socrates is articulating an early version of what would come to be called social contract theory, an understanding of political association as involving an agreement among individuals to abide by mutually binding rules and conventions. In such a social contract, the community gains the right, under certain conditions, to act against the individual's will and interest. In his brilliant elaboration of this idea, Jean-Jacques Rousseau proposed that political liberty consists precisely in obeying laws one has formulated as part of a social contract. These laws, which express the "general will," can be forcibly imposed on members of the social contract in what Rousseau famously described as being "forced to be free."[21]

But reading Socrates's argument, I can't help but feel that he overstates his case:

---

21. Jean-Jacques Rousseau, *The Basic Political Writings*, 2nd ed., translated and edited by Donald A. Cress (Indianapolis and Cambridge: Hackett Publishing Company, 2011), p. 167.

You must either persuade it [the city] or obey its orders, and endure in silence whatever it instructs you to endure, whether blows or bonds, and if it leads you into war to be wounded or killed, you must obey. To do so is right, and one must not give way or retreat or leave one's post, but both in war and in courts and everywhere else, one must obey the commands of one's city and country, or persuade it as to the nature of justice.[22]

Crito doesn't seem to have the will to argue, but Socrates's position isn't completely solid here. We remember that he himself told the Athenian jurors that if they commanded him to cease the practice of philosophy, he would not obey. We bristle at the thought of blind obedience to a government, remembering that governments are instituted among men to secure certain inalienable rights, that they derive their just powers from the consent of the governed, and that whenever any government becomes destructive to these ends, it is the right of the people to alter or abolish it. Or at least such were the claims made by an eighteenth-century British subject named Thomas Jefferson on behalf thirteen English settlements in North America. Socrates's position seems to leave no room for what Henry David Thoreau would call "resistance to civil government."

But there is another way of understanding Socrates's actions here, as Martin Luther King Jr. did in his "Letter from a Birmingham Jail." In this view, Socrates was engaging in a highly advanced form of non-violent civil disobedience in order to highlight the difference between what is legal and what is just. "I submit that an individual who breaks a law the conscience

---

22. *Trial and Death*, 51b.

tells him is unjust, and willingly accepts the penalty by staying in jail to arouse the conscience of the community over its injustice, is in reality expressing the highest respect for law."[23]

Socrates refused to give up philosophy and, in this way, contravened the will of his fellow citizens. His non-violent acceptance of the ultimate punishment is in effect the highest form of resistance, using what Mahatma Gandhi called "soul force" to bring into relief the moral deficiency of the law. Socrates's entire activity of philosophy was an investigation into the standard by which one could judge a law to be unjust. While never claiming to have attained ultimate answers, he did attain one clear conviction: that the pursuit of truth was right in itself and to be defended with one's very life.

There is a thread connecting Socrates, Jefferson, Thoreau, King, and Gandhi. The thread is long and winding, but you can trace it through texts that have survived to this day. Works through whose study one can keep track of this thread also find a place in my five-foot shelf and in my ideal general education curriculum.

o o o

One could say that the *Phaedo* is the least Socratic and the most Platonic of the three dialogues in my collection. It is dominated by metaphysical questions that, as far as we can tell, didn't much concern the historical Socrates. As in most of his dialogues, in the *Phaedo* Plato uses Socrates as a vehicle for pursuing his own philosophical preoccupations. The questions of the *Apology*

---

23. Martin Luther King Jr., "Letter from Birmingham Jail," in *The American Intellectual Tradition, Vol. II: 1865 to the Present*, David Hollinger and Charles Capper, eds., 5th ed. (New York and Oxford: Oxford University Press, 2006), p. 415.

and the *Crito* are primarily ethical—What is virtue? How do we live well?—whereas those dominating the *Phaedo* are metaphysical—What is it to be? What is it to know?

Many scholars place the *Apology* and the *Crito* among Plato's early dialogues, whereas the *Phaedo* comes from a middle period of more systematic philosophical thought. But if Plato composed the *Phaedo* sometime after the *Apology* and the *Crito*, and therefore quite some time after Socrates's execution, the *Phaedo* still throbs with the trauma of Socrates's death. If a long time had passed, Plato had not gotten over it. Whatever philosophical densities are stuffed into the dialogue, the *Phaedo* is a tribute to the old master from a pupil whose heart is still sore with grief.

The dialogue opens with Echecrates asking Phaedo, "Were you with Socrates yourself, Phaedo, on the day when he drank the poison in prison, or did someone else tell you about it?"[24] Phaedo responds that he was there and found the event "an astonishing experience." Echecrates wants to hear everything, and Phaedo is happy to oblige him, "for nothing gives me more pleasure than to call Socrates to mind, whether talking about him myself, or hearing someone else do so."[25]

Phaedo and a few other friends arrive at the jail at daybreak, before visitors are allowed in. The gatekeeper asks them to wait, as Socrates is at that moment being instructed on how the execution, which will take place at sunset that day, will proceed. After a short while, his friends are let in, and they find Xanthippe, Socrates's wife, already there with their infant son in her arms. Late in his life, Socrates had married a much younger Xanthippe, who bore him three sons. She's crying, and Socrates

---

24. *Trial and Death*, 57a.
25. *Trial and Death*, 58d.

asks Crito to have someone take her home. She's led away "lamenting and beating her breast."[26]

Plato leaves it to the reader to imagine those last moments of familial intimacy in the twilight of the approaching final day. Did Socrates deliver a philosophical argument, like he did to Crito, to explain why Xanthippe would have to fend for herself and raise their three sons alone? Did he hold his baby and kiss his neck and try to make him laugh one last time? Did he lift him in the air and utter a prayer to the gods, as Hector did with Astyanax before his fateful encounter with deadly Achilles? Did he give Xanthippe some last words for his teenage sons? Did he have some last words for her? Plato doesn't say but simply paints this seemingly unnecessary last portrait of home life. Why is that? It is, at least, an echo of the issue Crito raised earlier: the tension between domestic responsibilities and intellectual independence.

Plato's dialogues are full of humanizing vignettes like this that seem superfluous to a strictly philosophical reading. But to get the most out of Plato, you have to pay close attention to these casual details. They are, in fact, never trivial. Plato demands of his readers a literary sensibility alert to the aesthetic dimension of his philosophy.

Crito sends Xanthippe home with one of his servants, and her departure clears the ground for philosophizing. Her tears will be invoked again when the metaphysics end and Socrates drinks the poison. Trying—unsuccessfully—to put his friends at ease about his impending death, Socrates makes a series of arguments for the immortality of the soul. I already "believed" in the soul's immortality when I first read these arguments in

---

26. Plato, *Phaedo*, trans. by G.M.A Grube, 2nd ed. (Indianapolis: Hackett Publishing Company, 1977), 60b, p. 8.

high school and was eager to have Socrates's rational demon-strations confirm my belief. But they didn't. Though I could not refute it—I wasn't sure I could even follow it—I was not per-suaded by Socrates's reasoning. The arguments felt forced. They left me the same sort of cold that some evangelical doctrines were leaving me, despite my efforts to believe. As Emily Dick-inson put it in her acid way—

Believing what we don't believe
Does not exhilarate.

Not even his friends were convinced, as evidenced by the outbreak of tears and sobs as the sun sets and the moment to drink the poison arrives. But even if this ostensibly central set of arguments fails to persuade, the *Phaedo* remains philosophi-cally important in many ways, including the fact that it contains one of Plato's most detailed presentations of his so-called The-ory of Forms, the understanding that anchors all of his metaphysics.

o o o

Metaphysics is a curious thing. The brain resists it. It usually takes prodding to make our minds perform the kind of contor-tion that brings metaphysical questions into focus. Simply try-ing to define "metaphysics" dumps you into metaphysical quicksand. The plain (that is, the *Merriam-Webster Collegiate Dictionary*, 11th edition) definition is a useful starting point: "a division of philosophy that is concerned with the fundamental nature of reality and being." But what can those words—"the fundamental nature of reality and being"—refer to? The dic-tionary can't help us there. What can those words mean? What does the mind grasp when it grasps their meaning?

When we ask about the fundamental nature of reality and being, we are also necessarily asking about our capacity to know anything about such a thing. Knowing anything about the fundamental nature of reality suggests that one aspect of that reality (our minds) can stand apart from the broader thing and assimilate it into itself in the special way we call "knowing." But nothing can stand apart from reality and grasp it as an object of knowledge; everything, including the "knowing" and the agent that does the "knowing," has to be included in "reality." Knowing anything about the fundamental nature of reality and being, then, would have to be a kind of self-consciousness, since the thing that knows must itself be part of the reality it knows. The mind swoons.

Plato is, above all, a metaphysician, and almost everything he argues comes back in one way or another to some aspect of the Theory of Forms. When I try to explain the Theory of Forms to students who may never have encountered it before, I ask them to imagine a perfect circle. Everyone is able to do this without difficulty. Then I point out that no one has ever actually seen a perfect circle—every circle we experience with our physical senses will contain some imperfection or irregularity, even if it's so minute that we fail to perceive it. The same goes for a straight line—no one has ever seen one. These things exist, says Plato, only as objects of the intellect. They exist as Forms—accessible to the intellect but not to the senses. What the senses perceive are approximations or imitations of these perfect entities. For Plato, this holds true not just for geometrical figures but for everything. Reality as perceived by the senses is an imperfect imitation of something that exists in perfect, immutable, and eternal Form in the realm of ideas. This realm of Forms is what is, in fact, real, and what we perceive through the physical senses is illusory, like shadows on a wall. To know something, then, is to know its Form.

Think of a chair. There are many kinds of chairs—folding chairs, sofa chairs, desk chairs, wooden chairs, paintings of chairs, imaginary chairs, the word "chair." What makes all of these objects chairs is their resemblance to some sort of Ideal Chair, or the Form Chair. In Plato's formulation, all chairs "participate" in the Form Chair; they are more perfect or more defective depending on their distance from the Form. A well-constructed chair will be closer to the Form than a badly made one, and a badly made chair, in turn, will be closer to the Form than a chair you see in a picture or read about in a book. Forms are the true objects of knowledge, and to attain them, one has to transcend the realm of the senses. Forms themselves, in turn, exist by virtue of their participation in what we can think of as the Form of Form and which Plato calls the Form of the Good. Christian theologians, especially Saint Augustine, would come to identify this ultimate Form, from which all being emanates, with the Christian God.

For the most part, a normal person is not urgently concerned with metaphysics. It strikes one as intellectual humbug, easily dismissed with the simple question "So what?" But metaphysical issues are actually unavoidable. No matter how distant they seem from the immediate concerns of our lives, we cannot help but bump into them from time to time, as against guardrails of what's thinkable.

We often look the other way when we face metaphysical conundrums. They are harder to avoid if you have serious conversations with small children, who tend to be keenly interested in metaphysical questions, like the child who asked Walt Whitman, "What is the grass?" or my two-year-old, who asked me, "What is the mind?" But even when we successfully avoid metaphysics, we only do so by relying on unconscious metaphysical assumptions. We cannot have any standard of right and wrong, truth and falsity, for example, except by positing some metaphysical anchor point. Even for someone who places self-interest as the only standard of right and wrong, truth and falsity, the question remains of how self-interest is to be determined, since that idea already implies a notion of an ultimate good.

It's not uncommon for conversations in liberal arts classrooms to skid into metaphysical territory. These moments can be intellectually thrilling and offer a glimpse into a kind of mystery that comes interwoven with our everyday experience. Philosophy asks difficult and extraordinary questions that take us to the edge of what is knowable and tries to penetrate them with rigor and honesty.

The *Phaedo* asks such questions. Not all of the answers satisfy, but the simple notion that issues such as the nature of existence, the soul, and the human good are subject to rational investigation, not merely religious decrees, is exhilarating all on its own. Early in the dialogue, Socrates claims that "the one aim of those who practice philosophy in the proper manner is to practice for dying and death."[27] What Socrates calls here the proper practice of philosophy is not what typically happens in a graduate philosophy seminar, but it is very much what happens in a liberal arts classroom. To practice liberal education is to always keep ultimate questions in view, grappling ever more intimately with the fact of our mortality. Any inquiry into the meaning of a human life—the nature of its good—must propose a view on death. In the *Phaedo*, as elsewhere, Socrates insists that the investigation into the human good, and its

---

27. *Trial and Death*, 64a.

attendant attention to the question of death, is itself a key element of the virtuous life. As he put it in the *Apology,* "It is the
greatest good for a man to discuss virtue every day."[28]

o o o

The word "virtue" in contemporary English carries many con-
notations that aren't there in the Greek word Socrates used—
arete. In its most basic sense, *arete* simply means excellence. To
think about *arete* as applied to a human life means to think
about the nature of human excellence, or the human good.

As Aristotle points out in the opening of the *Ethics,* everyone
agrees that the good at which human life aims is called happiness, but there is little agreement as to what, exactly, happiness
is.[29] The *Ethics* is Aristotle's deep dive into the subject. The word
he uses is *eudaimonia,* for which the English word "happiness"
doesn't provide a perfect translation. Some translators prefer the
phrase "human flourishing," since when Aristotle describes *eudaimonia* he speaks of an ongoing manner of living, a kind of
good fortune that results from one's deliberate actions. In contrast to our common notion of happiness, Aristotle thinks of
eudaimonia as an activity rather than as a state. You cannot attain
eudaimonia as the passive recipient of good experiences. The
flourishing life involves activity and, in particular, activity that
displays *arete,* or excellence. And what sort of thing is *human*
excellence? For Aristotle, human excellence involves the use of
what he takes to be our peculiar human capacity: reason.[30]

---

28. *Trial and Death,* 38a.

29. Aristotle, *The Nicomachean Ethics,* Oxford World Classics, Oxford University
Press, Oxford and New York, 2009, 1095a, 18–20.

30. *Nicomachean Ethics,* 1097b, 22–1098a, 1–8.

The centrality Aristotle accords to the cultivation of reason in his conception of a good life leads him to reflect on the kind of education that is most conducive to such cultivation. The kind of education he describes is what we have come to call liberal education. He turns to the topic in his book on *Politics*, which he produced as a companion treatise to the *Ethics*, since every political community can be understood as an attempt to create the conditions for the attainment of *eudaimonia*: "It comes to be for the sake of living, but it remains in existence for the sake of living well."[31]

Liberal education, in Aristotle's view, can simply be defined as that education which is appropriate for a free individual. Toward the end of the *Politics*, he writes: "It is evident, then, that there is a certain kind of education that children must be given not because it is useful or necessary but because it is noble and suitable for a free person," adding that "it is completely inappropriate for magnanimous and free people to be always asking what use something is."[32]

This ancient conception of liberal education as the education that is suitable for a free person is especially meaningful in contemporary society, where we have enshrined individual liberty as the central value of our political order. It is not as simple an idea as it seems at first blush. One implication immediately stands out. What the ancients meant by a "free person" includes not only what today we would call *political* freedom, but also what we would think of as *economic* freedom. That is, to be a free person, one has to be free, to some extent, from what Aristotle calls "vulgar" work, or "work done for wages."[33] He

31. Aristotle, *Politics*, C.D.C. Reeve, trans. (Indianapolis and Cambridge: Hackett Publishing Company, 1998), 1252b, 29.

32. *Politics*, 1138a, 29–31, 1338b, 2–3.

33. *Politics*, 1337b, 12–13.

drives the point home when discussing the nature of political citizenship: "The best city-state will not confer citizenship on vulgar craftsmen. . . . For it is impossible to engage in virtuous pursuits while living the life of a vulgar craftsman or hired laborer."[34] While we would reject the notion that only a leisured class is suited for political citizenship, we can't dismiss the point that democratic self-governance requires a kind of cultivation among citizens that can only happen when they don't devote all of their energy to earning a living. In Aristotle's words, a citizen's virtue (*arete*) requires that one be "freed from necessary tasks";[35] it requires the capacity for "leisured activity" or *schole*, from which we derive the word "school."

Rights and equality before the law mean little in a democracy unless individuals have the scope to develop their humanity in a way that is free from the yoke of economic compulsion. When we think about liberal education today, we should be thinking about the portion of a student's education that is not concerned with moneymaking, the portion that asks students to think not about what job they want to have, but about what kind of life they want to live. In his extraordinary 1903 collection of essays *The Souls of Black Folk*, W.E.B. Du Bois made this very point with reference to the education that was appropriate for an American black population recently emancipated from slavery: "The true college will ever have one goal," he wrote, "not to earn meat, but to know the end and aim of the life which meat nourishes."[36]

---

34. *Politics*, 1278a, 7, 20–21.

35. *Politics*, 1278, 9–10.

36. W.E.B. Du Bois, *The Souls of Black Folk*, Henry Louis Gates Jr. and Terri Hume Oliver, eds., Norton Critical Edition (New York and London: W. W. Norton, 1999), p. 58.

This point is particularly important and particularly unintuitive. It's an especially awkward idea for students and families who are looking at college as a way to escape poverty and marginality. It was an uphill battle for W.E.B. Du Bois to argue for a place for Shakespeare and Marcus Aurelius in the education of blacks facing the violence and exploitation of Jim Crow in the aftermath of slavery. Today, too, it is difficult to impress on economically anxious families, many of them incurring significant debts to pay for college, that a liberal education is not a frivolous distraction from a useful education, but the very thing that will give purpose and direction to a useful education.

o o o

What the content of a liberal education should be is typically a subject of much contention among college faculties. In fact, the going assumption is that consensus on this question is impossible, so universities have resorted to prescribing learning outcomes in terms of skills and competencies, letting faculty decide how they want to meet these content-free goals. Together with the emphasis on skills over content, the widespread use of distribution requirements as a way of "fulfilling" the liberal portion of a college education means, in effect, that very little institutional energy or vision goes into specifying what a liberal education is, even in places that proudly proclaim themselves to be liberal arts colleges.

Yet understanding liberal education as education for freedom has immediate implications about content. One implication is that a liberal education should concern itself with reflection on the nature of human excellence or the human good—what the Greeks called "virtue." An obvious way to pursue this broad question is through courses in which students encounter works that, over a long period of time, have proved especially potent catalysts for reflection on the fundamental question of the human good. One name given to such works is "classics."

As almost everyone who has experienced it will confirm, a liberal education based on the study of works of major histori-cal and cultural significance confers an inexhaustible treasure that you carry with you for the rest of your life. There are, of course, far more works of this type than can be included in any curriculum, so judicious selection sensitive to contemporary contexts and concerns must still be made. The curriculum of an American university, for instance, calls for a different selection of material than, say, a Chinese or Indian university. A technical college, a religious college, a historically black college, and a traditional liberal arts college will all bring different concerns and traditions to the choice of texts to be included in a common curriculum. Similarly, our contemporary awareness of issues like race, gender, and colonialism should inform our judgments about which works from the past are most conducive to a lib-eral education today. Yet, in all cases, works that grapple with the core questions of politics, religion, and philosophy that have shaped our world deserve a prominent place in general education. The aim of such an education is not to provide an-swers to these fundamental questions, but to bring them to life for the student and to instill habits or reflection and inquiry that can serve as guides for life.

o o o

The recognition that liberal education involves the search for genuine self-knowledge sometimes motivates the idea that when students arrive at college, they should be exposed to works that affirm their identity, works in which they can "see themselves." This strikes me as a correct intuition. But we have to guard against too narrow a conception of what sorts of identities our students bring with them and what aspects of it we should affirm. In the United States, with its history of racial oppression and ethnic diversity, many people have embraced the notion that the works and authors included in a common curriculum must represent the demographic diversity of the student body. A curriculum might be representative of works produced in a given time period, in a given genre, or on a given topic, but representation of the cultural backgrounds of a diverse student body as an organizing principle in general education necessarily leads to incoherence, essentialism, and tokenism. Although courses that respond to and reflect the diversity of the student body are essential offerings, the criterion of democratic representation—appropriate for politics—is not appropriate for selecting common curricula; to adopt it as such is to abandon the very idea of education and to turn students into interest groups, each lobbying for their own special curricular accommodations.

For me, arriving at Columbia as a freshman in 1991 meant the discovery of myself as an ethnic subject—a figure who, walking around campus, eating in the dining halls, and sitting in a seminar room, symbolized something that was until then unknown to me. It took me a long time to begin to make sense of the landscape in which my mere presence as a poor person of color at an Ivy League institution had a political meaning. When I arrived at Columbia, I didn't know that I registered to those around me as a member of an oppressed minority who was socially disadvantaged. I didn't know that my presence at Columbia was evidence of its institutional commitment to something called "diversity." I had all these aspects of identity foisted on me before I knew what they were. In this, as in other ways, I was disoriented; I did not understand what, for most of my peers, went without saying.

I quickly came to resent expectations about who I was supposed to be, what I was supposed to like, what political views I was supposed to hold, what student groups I was supposed to join, what classes and topics I was supposed to be interested in, what identity I was supposed to need affirmed. It was at Columbia, coming subtly from faculty and administrators and overtly from my peers of color, that I first became aware of being treated on the basis of other people's idea of what my skin color and my ethnicity meant. Even to this day, I have to counter the assumption that since I am an academic, I must be the resident expert on Latino studies. "No," I say, "my doctoral work was on New England Transcendentalists and the abolitionist movement, and in recent years, I've also focused on the meaning and practice of liberal education."

This is all to say that we professors too often have a preconceived notion of our students' identities and of what should feel true to them. A liberal education can only take place when those notions are held lightly and seen through. As a young person trying to understand what it meant to be who I was and to be where I was, I found in Plato a genuine affirmation of my identity. It was not my identity as a Dominican immigrant that Socrates affirmed, but something more fundamental, an identity that cut me loose from the assumptions of my peers at Columbia as much as it did from the expectations of my Dominican community. I took to heart Socrates's innocent and saccharine admonitions. They pointed toward what felt like the most worthwhile way of living for me. Here was a sort of identity that felt true to my deepest self. Here was the life of the mind—a way of living that held out the possibility of absorbing the disparate parts of who I was into some kind of integrated whole.

CHAPTER 3

Making Peace with the Unconscious: Freud

Along with Socrates, who admonished Athenians to live examined lives, and Augustine, who turned his attention to himself to discover the ultimate truths of Christianity, Sigmund Freud's primary concern was with self-knowledge. Twenty-five hundred years after Plato, and fifteen hundred years after Augustine, he pursued his investigation using the intellectual tools of modern science and framed his theories within the medical discourse of his day. He left behind a mixed and contested legacy. But in the pantheon of thinkers, ancient and modern, who have shaped our understanding of the human mind, Freud holds his own. For me and many of my students, his ideas and provocations have led to far-reaching insights and personal transformations.

I'm not sure if I had heard of Freud before college. My first clear memory of his name comes from the six-week academic boot camp required by the Higher Education Opportunity Program (HEOP), through which I had been admitted to Columbia. That was in July 1991. Along with literature, writing, and math, the HEOP summer curriculum included a course in psychology taught by Dr. Jama Adams, who was also a practicing psychologist. I had never laid eyes on a psychologist in real life, and the idea that Dr. Adams could have special insight into the mind—and that people revealed to him their intimate lives—made him an object of fascination.

My idea of a psychologist came, primarily, from an immensely popular call-in radio show called *El psiquiatra en su hogar* ("The Psychiatrist in Your Home") that played in the Dominican Republic in the mid-1980s. Dr. Máximo Beras Goico (*el psiquiatra*) offered flash consultations on the air. Armed with rational and scientific common sense, he fielded all kinds of questions from all kinds of people. It was a national education hour. He took on old wives' tales, folk traditions, superstition, and plain prejudice. He was combative, funny, penetrating, and the most learned person I had ever heard speak. He never mentioned Freud or the unconscious, but it was common for people to call in about one thing, and, lo, their real problem would turn out to be something entirely different, something they didn't realize or hadn't wanted to talk about but which the astute doctor was able to draw out. Those were the best calls. It seemed to me that sometimes he could hear things that rest of us, including the person speaking, did not realize were being said. And this special skill, this secret power that was not magic or religion, had struck me as an amazing thing.

In this way, I was prepared—or unprepared—for Freud.

In the HEOP program, teaching my cohort of Columbia students-to-be, Dr. Adams would sometimes talk about his own clinical practice. The thick psychology textbook he assigned for the class made for engrossing reading. His lectures were my first big thrill of college. Early in the class, perhaps on the first day, he introduced Freud by saying something that took firm hold of my mind: "The reasons we give ourselves for doing the things that we do are never the real reasons."

At eighteen, I knew that my motives for doing the things I did, or for believing the things I believed, or for wanting the things I wanted, had a way of shifting from under me. Sometimes new and unsuspected reasons would come into view, like the silhouette of objects emerging from darkness at daybreak. They had been there all along, in front of me, but shrouded in unconsciousness. When I had thought I was being strictly scrupulous and reasonable, I might later come to realize that I was being hostile and vindictive. When I had thought that I was *really, honestly* indifferent, I might later discover that I was, in fact, inwardly crushed. Those vague intuitions had now found distinct expression: "The reasons we give ourselves for doing the things that we do are never the real reasons."

o o o

In lecture eighteen of his 1917 *Introductory Lectures on Psycho-Analysis*, Freud identified three "major blows" delivered by science to humanity's "naive self-love." The first blow was the discovery that the earth was not at the center of the universe. Instead, our planet, like the others, circled the sun from a location that had no obvious significance. The unsettling realization that the universe did not feature the earth as its focal point changed nothing about how people went about their everyday lives, but it also changed everything. This understanding is so common today that it takes effort to imagine just how disturbing the revelation would have been to people accustomed to thinking of themselves as God's special concern. It was not well-received by religious authorities.

The second blow delivered by science doubled down on the notion that humans were not as special as they thought. By the mid-nineteenth century, a vast array of evidence had been collected pointing to the fact that human beings emerged, like other species, through a process of gradual evolution by natural selection. We came about in fits and starts, guided by nothing but the need to survive an unforgiving "struggle for existence," as Charles Darwin called the third chapter of his monumental "long argument," *The Origin of Species*. What Darwin demonstrated in 1859—even as three-year-old Sigmund Schlomo Freud, over in Moravia, grappled with the Oedipal complexities of his nuclear family—was not, as is popularly believed, that humans descended from apes but, far more disconcertingly, that humans *are* apes.

We associate the first of Freud's "blows" with Nicolaus Copernicus and the observations of Galileo Galilei at the turn of the seventeenth century. The second blow we associate with Darwin. The third blow was delivered by Freud himself. It concerns the psychoanalytic "discovery" of the unconscious or, more precisely, the idea that who and what we are is primarily determined by unconscious mental processes. Freud, who has never been accused of excessive modesty or understatement, considered this the "most wounding blow" of the three, coming to "disturb the peace of this world" and the "megalomania" of our species.

According to Freud, not only are we not at the center of the universe, and not only are we not biologically special, but we are not even masters of our own minds. We are not transparent to ourselves. We do not command our thoughts, our desires, the psychic forces that shape us; they come to us from a place we do not know. The conscious self operates on the illusion of self-transparency, of self-command, of being what it is by virtue of

its awareness of itself. But alas, Freud tells us, the whole appara-
tus is an illusion, an elaborate mechanism of self-deception.

When introducing Freud to students, I like to point out that
the lack of self-determination in our conscious mind is evident
in everyday experience. Whenever the mind is not occupied
with some external stimulus like reading, conversation, or a
screen, it will wander; it will not stay in place or remain blank.
Like nature, the mind abhors a vacuum. As you walk or drive
from, say, your home to the grocery store, thoughts will come
in a continuous stream, with no gaps in between them. The vast
majority of them you will hardly notice, though you can make
a point of observing your thoughts, practicing the watchful attentiveness that's often called "mindfulness." But even for experienced practitioners of mindfulness meditation, it's almost
impossible to sustain this watchfulness for long; you will soon
be "lost" in thought, riding a train whose origin, destination,
and conductor you do not know. Your mind will be generating
memories, plans, intentions, fantasies—verbal and nonverbal—
each sliding into the other seamlessly, following some enigmatic logic of association. When this experience becomes pronounced, we aptly call it daydreaming because of its similarity
to the mental events we remember having experienced while
asleep.

In Freud's understanding, the mind is *driven*, and the conscious "I" is not the driver. Our self-command, which tends to
feel absolute, is, in fact, always profoundly compromised
because the controlling forces in our mind are inaccessible to
us. The mythical image of the centaur captures our situation: a
human head and torso emerging from the body of a wild horse.
The human part, our conscious self, has the power of speech
and reason, but the horse on which it sits is a wild beast, the
bringer, as in the ancient myths, of chaos, mayhem, and

unbridled lust. They are not two, but one. The beast cannot know itself except by means of its rational protrusion, which is not beast anymore, but a self-conscious agent. However, this agent believes itself to be an autonomous actor and knows nothing of the beast from which it draws its vitality and where all of its life functions are organized.

The conscious sense of self, the "ego," is the proverbial tip of the iceberg: the tiny outcrop of an immense mass of unconscious mental processes that constitutes who and what we are.[1]

According to Freud, unconscious material breaks through into the open on a regular basis, but always disguised and unrecognizable to the conscious mind for what it really is. These occurrences disrupt our normal mental operations and commonly manifest as "errors," or, in the stilted translation of the authorized standard edition of Freud's works, "parapraxes." These are the mundane mistakes and foibles that punctuate our everyday lives: slips of the tongue, hearing something other than what was said, forgetting a name or a word, misplacing an object, dialing the wrong number, hitting "reply all" when you only mean to respond to the sender.

Freud argued that these "errors" are neither random nor meaningless, as is readily admitted at least in some cases. A favorite example of Freud's was when the President of the Lower House of the Austrian Parliament, at the opening of a particularly contentious session, brought down the gavel and declared that the session was officially *closed*. What's funny about this

---

1. Freud identified the conscious sense of self with the German first-person pronoun, *Ich*. In the authorized English translation, instead of the English equivalent "I," Freud approved of the Latin translation "ego," reaching, as he always was, for scientific exactitude. Hence, his famous structural model comes to us in English as dividing the mind into ego, id, and superego, rather than the straightforward English translations of the German terms: "I," "it," and "super-I."

slip is precisely that it is not meaningless; it expresses a fantasy that the President of Parliament would find embarrassing and which he would perhaps not admit even to himself: the wish that the contentious session of parliament he is opening would instead be closing.

In his popular 1904 book *The Psychopathology of Everyday Life*, Freud presented a plethora of examples of slips that were errors only in the sense that they said something other than what the speaker intended; but they were not errors at all in that they revealed a deeper truth about the speaker's state of mind. Another favorite example of his is that of a lady "well-known for her energy" who reports that when her husband asked his doctor what diet he should follow, the doctor said the husband did not need to follow any diet at all—in other words, said the lady, "He could eat and drink whatever I want."

The significance of these revelatory errors suggested to Freud that "the slip of the tongue may perhaps itself have a right to be regarded as a completely valid psychical act, pursuing an aim of its own, as a statement with a content and significance."[2] Freud argued further that it is not only these relatively rare instances of slips that have significance; in fact, *all* such "errors" do. They are all leaks from the unconscious.

Freud worked out this novel theory of how the unconscious becomes manifest through his work with neurotic patients. At the turn of the eighteenth century, patients suffering from neurotic illnesses went to see doctors who, like Freud, specialized in neurological disorders. The catch-all name for these neurotic conditions was "hysteria." Cases of hysteria appeared in myriad

---

2. Sigmund Freud, *Introductory Lectures on Psycho-Analysis*, Vol. 15 in the *Standard Edition of the Complete Psychological Works of Sigmund Freud*, edited and translated by James Strachey (London: Hogarth Press, 1958), p. 34.

forms. Their defining feature was that the symptoms had no detectable organic origin and often did not correspond to any underlying physiological function.

Freud had returned to Vienna in February 1886 to open his medical practice after spending five months in Paris studying under the renowned neurologist Jean-Martin Charcot. At the time, Charcot was showing dramatic results in the treatment of hysteria through the use of hypnosis. His striking demonstrations left Freud in awe—Charcot could not only induce hysterical symptoms like paralysis on normal people (any magic-show hypnotist could do that), but he could also remove such symptoms from true hysterics.

Back in Vienna, around the same time, Freud's close friend and mentor, the eminent neurophysiologist Josef Breuer, was himself experimenting with hypnosis to treat the bizarre collection of symptoms plaguing a young patient named Bertha Pappenheim. Although Freud never treated Pappenheim and only heard about the case from Breuer, Freud identifies her as the founding patient of psychoanalysis. The case formed the centerpiece of the book he and Breuer published in 1895, *Studies in Hysteria*, where she was identified as "Anna O."

The key breakthrough in Anna O's case was the discovery of certain disturbing memories that she had expunged from her awareness and which, when recovered under hypnosis, provided relief from her strange symptoms.[3] A further detail became the key to Freud's understanding of the unconscious: the peculiar way in which Anna's symptoms resembled the repressed memories. For example, Anna's inability to drink water was relieved

---

3. Subsequent research has cast serious doubt on whether Anna O. ever experienced any real relief from her condition. Irrespective of this, the clues Freud drew from the case opened the door to the entire theory of psychoanalysis.

by the memory of her deep but unexpressed disgust at seeing a dog lapping water from the glass of a lady she disliked. The paralysis on the left side of her body could be traced to a terrifying memory in which, dozing off while sitting next to her ailing father, she had a hallucination of a snake emerging from behind the bed but found herself unable to drive it away because her arm had become numb from hanging over the back of the chair.

It dawned on Freud that hysterical symptoms were, in fact, disguised expressions of wishes, fantasies, and memories that had been split off from awareness because they were, in one way or another, unacceptable. The repressed material would break forth as a symptom. And thus hysterical symptoms held a *signifying* relation to the repressed mental content from which they originated. The doctor's task was to interpret the symptom so as to arrive at its unconscious root and then bring the patient to a better and less incapacitating experience of the repressed material. The more Freud followed this approach in the treatment of hysterical symptoms, the vaster the realm into which it opened appeared to be. Unconscious mental constructs turned out to be not marginal and incidental aspects of our mental life, but constitutive and dominant.

And so came into the world the third great wound to man's narcissistic self-regard.

o o o

Freud has been given a bad rap. When introducing him to sophomores in the Contemporary Civilization course, I often begin by asking them whether any of them have read Freud before. Few have. I then ask them to tell me what they know about Freud. Invariably, one of the first comments I get, often from a

Psychology major, is that Freud's theories have been discredited and are not taken seriously in academic psychology. It's true. Like Marx, whose work as an economist is virtually ignored in Economics departments, Freud's influence exists largely outside of the discipline in which he understood himself to be working.

But Freudian thought is pervasive. Unlike many other major thinkers, his views have fully penetrated popular culture. People who have never heard of Freud regularly make use of his vocabulary and his concepts. Sit at a bar or anywhere there is free-flowing conversation, and it won't be long before you hear Freud whispering from within the words of the people speaking: someone's ego might be singled out as problematic; Freudian slips might be noted and Oedipal complexes invoked; you might hear speculations about how someone's personality quirks are rooted in childhood trauma, or how the narcissism of today's youth will destroy our country. If you find the whole thing to be too much, someone might recommend you get therapy.

Part of the infectiousness of Freudian thinking comes from his skill as a writer. Freud is fun to read and fun to think about. He is always eager to shock and scandalize you and force you to reconsider something that, on its face, strikes you as absurd. Almost anything that Freud wrote invites the reader into self-analysis, to consider psychic structures that are exceedingly hard to see precisely because they are the lenses *through* which we see. And, of course, the prominence he attached to sex happened to work as a master stroke of marketing. Or, rather, the unequaled effectiveness of sex-signaling in marketing—no matter how antiseptic the product—supports Freud's notion that it is everywhere you look in the mind.

As with other influential thinkers, one should not read Freud as presenting ultimate truths. In other words, the most productive way of approaching Freud in a liberal arts context is to uncover his fundamental ideas and wrestle with their significance without getting entangled in his often tendentious theoretical and clinical elaborations.

The text I usually teach as an introduction to Freud is a small book based on lectures he gave in 1909 during his only visit to America and published in the standard edition as *Five Lectures on Psycho-Analysis*. I teach it immediately after Nietzsche's *Genealogy of Morals*. It's a tricky juxtaposition, because after Nietzsche's raw and elemental force, Freud can seem tame. But where Nietzsche is a bolt of lightning, Freud is an electrical current; where Nietzsche is an exploding geyser, Freud is a steam engine.

o o o

The contrast between Freud's ambiguous place in academic psychology and his enormous value in general education illustrates an important feature of liberal learning: its tendency to run against the prevalent disciplinary currents and intellectual vogues in academia. The practice of liberal education, especially in the context of a research university, is pointedly countercultural. For the typical faculty member in a top university, undergraduate general education represents a kind of professional backwater, a form of "service" with little to negative value in the ladder of professorial prestige . This is all the more pronounced in general education programs that focus on the study of "canonical" texts. Works that have decisively shaped the evolution of our dominant social institutions—including the university itself—are often treated in academia as contaminated objects, purveyors of the prejudices and injustices that afflict our society. This ideological hostility to the "great books" has been one important contributor to the weakening of general education in recent decades.

The story of how the place of liberal education became so precarious in the modern university can be told from many angles, but a few things are evident across the board. One is that the erosion of humanistic learning of the kind that I found in the Columbia Core Curriculum and which still, not without difficulty, persists there, is directly linked to the rise of the "research university" and the dominance of what Anthony Kronman has called "the research ideal" in higher education.[4]

The research university is a breathtaking cultural achievement. Its roots can be traced to reforms in the nineteenth-century German university led by Wilhelm von Humboldt, who founded the University of Berlin in 1809. The organizing idea behind the research university is straightforward: an institution dedicated to the production, accumulation, and dissemination of knowledge. By the mid-nineteenth century, the research university had become the banner vehicle for the Enlightenment ideas we associate with the "scientific revolution" and with figures like Francis Bacon and René Descartes. Objectivity, verifiability, and the experimental method became the hallmarks for what could be properly considered knowledge.

To put it in its most elementary terms, the driving force behind the rise of the research university has been the triumph of modern science. The scientific model of research dominates the university and has proved its value again and again. Modernity, as we know it, has been made and remade through the

---

4. In the third chapter of his book *Education's End: Why Our Colleges and Universities Have Given Up on the Meaning of Life* (New Haven: Yale University Press, 2008), Kronman gives a historical account of the development of this ideal and of how it is implicated in the decline of secular humanism in the academy.

discoveries, inventions, and innovations produced through scientific research. Though I am a humanist by training and conviction, the primacy of science in the university strikes me as entirely justified and appropriate.

Yet the research enterprise of the modern university is not aimed at the cultivation of whole persons. Its central preoccupation is with the production and accumulation of new knowledge. Liberal education, on the other hand, concerns itself with the subjective experience of being human and with the basic character of the human good. These very terms sit uncomfortably in the epistemic regime that rules the research university. In my ten years as Director of the Center for the Core Curriculum at Columbia College, I worked and taught in the crucible of this tension. Indeed, the entire institutional history of Columbia University can be told through the tensions between the original College and the protean University that formed around it. And this is not unique to Columbia. Many of the leading universities in the United States emerged from colleges that had been dedicated to the training of young men for various forms of leadership but which came to see this quaint mission as an antiquated burden.

Like in the ancient myth of Oedipus, the college gave birth to the university, and the university has ever since been trying to kill its parent. At Columbia, President A. P. Barnard proposed outright in 1889 that the College be abolished. Though the motion failed before the Trustees, Columbia *College* faced repeated attempts at its dissolution as Columbia *University* took shape around it.[5] At about the same time, over at Harvard, President Charles W. Eliot was weighing the advice of historian

---

5. The best account of this period in the history of Columbia College is Lionel Trilling's essay "The Van Amringe and Keppel Eras," in *A History of Columbia College on Morningside* (New York: Columbia University Press, 1954).

Edward Channing, who proposed that "the College ought to be suppressed or moved out into the country where it would not interfere with the proper work of the University."[6] At the University of Chicago, as Robert Hutchins acknowledged in his 1929 inaugural address, "members of the Faculty have urged that we withdraw from undergraduate work, or at least the first two years of it."[7] Johns Hopkins, which was founded in 1876 and is widely recognized as the first fully developed American research university, was initially conceived without an undergraduate college at all.

There are other examples that illustrate that while many colleges live within universities and gain extraordinary advantages from them, the two institutions have always been at odds: the university is a center of research and innovation, while the college is a center of teaching and self-actualization. Columbia College Dean Herbert Hawkes noted in 1922 that *"the student is the focus of the undergraduate college,"*[8] with an implicit contrast to the university, where the focus was on the subject or on the academic discipline. In his book on the American college, Andrew Delbanco put it succinctly: "[The college] is about transmitting knowledge of and from the past to undergraduate students so they may draw upon it as a living resource in the future. [The university] is mainly an array of research activities conducted by faculty and graduate students with the aim of creating new knowledge in order to supersede the past."[9]

---

6. Robert McCaughey, *Stand, Columbia: A History of Columbia University in the City of New York, 1754–2004* (New York: Columbia University Press, 2003), p. 170.

7. Quoted in Daniel Bell, *The Reforming of General Education: The Columbia Experience in Its National Setting* (New York: Columbia University Press, 1966), p. 29.

8. Quoted in Bell, 1966, p. 24; the emphasis is mine.

9. Andrew Delbanco, *College: What It Was, Is, and Should Be* (Princeton: Princeton University Press, 2012), p. 2.

The research ideal in the academy has extended even to the practice of liberal education. Academic careers, even in the liberal arts, are made through "research," with monographs, articles, and conference papers serving as the principal measures of achievement. One of the results of this system of professional incentives is the production, in the liberal arts disciplines, of ever larger quantities of published research for ever narrower audiences. In the sciences, the research ideal has generally led to more effective accumulation and dissemination of knowledge; in the humanities and humanistic social sciences, it has generally meant fragmentation of expertise and withdrawal from the human questions that breathe life and meaning into the liberal arts. Because these questions are only marginally susceptible to scientific investigation, the research orientation of the academic profession ensures that they are largely neglected.

It's true that nearly all undergraduate programs will require a number of general education courses for the bachelor's degree, but when you scratch beneath the surface of the catalog descriptions, you typically find *departmental* courses, rooted in disciplinary specializations, with perhaps some tweaks here and there to justify their being offered as *general* education. True general education has been virtually squeezed out of the curriculum by the dominance of disciplinary specialization and the organization of universities into corresponding academic research departments.

Many colleges now think about liberal education simply as exposure to a range of academic disciplines, turning their general education requirement into a recipe for how many and how varied a set of academic disciplines a student must sample before graduation. But in important ways, liberal education must be non-disciplinary. As Jacques Barzun pointed out after a lifetime in both liberal education and university administration, "To be of any worth, the liberal arts . . . must also be taught as arts, not as scholarly disciplines—and that must be done by teachers. The present system, which favors faculty research over teaching, turns the liberal arts into professional subjects."[10]

Liberal education begins from the premise that the fundamental issues facing a student are not scholarly but existential; its basic mission is not epistemological but ethical. This does not negate the fact that a good part of a college education, especially today, must concern itself with preparing economically productive individuals who can perform specialized functions in society. But that's not the soul of the college. College must also be an oasis from the economic and technological forces that shape and distort our social institutions. Only from such a place can one understand and critically assess these forces.

The idea of a non-professionalizing education can sound very strange today. It's an idea starkly at odds with the market values that dominate in our culture. Every summer, when I teach my low-income high school students, I get puzzled looks when I first propose that the point of college isn't to prepare them to get good jobs. Many students—and their families— can't imagine what else could possibly be the point. I confess that it is hard to *tell* them what the point is. It is, in fact, almost impossible to communicate the meaning of a liberal education through arguments and admonitions. The difficulty is compounded when students come to college looking to escape poverty and marginality.

But what works with everyone else is what works with low-income high school students: *doing* liberal education. Contagion

---

10. Jacques Barzun, "Trim the College?—A Utopia!" *Chronicle of Higher Education* (June 22, 2001).

is the only effective method of communicating its value. The process is one of transmission rather than instruction. After three weeks in which we meet for two hours each day to discuss ancient, Enlightenment, and contemporary philosophical texts, I don't have to tell these "disadvantaged" students about the value of a liberal education. They know. They have had an experience that cannot be easily summarized, packaged, or reduced to instrumental value. They have certainly acquired new skills and accumulated a lot of new knowledge, but more importantly, they have tapped into inner capacities that have bearing on their entire lives—not only what they learn and what they do, but who they become.

o o o

My critique of the influence of the research ideal on liberal education should not be understood as denying the value of research in the liberal arts. Whether archival research, or work on original manuscripts, or unearthing new information about an author or text, research enriches our understanding of whatever material we use to conduct liberal education. It is an essential part of the life of the scholar. But the research ideal remains of limited value in undergraduate general education, and its dominance in the university and in the academic career has been detrimental to liberal education. A good deal of the contemporary "crisis" in the liberal arts stems from the institutional and professional landscape in which they operate. Research should have a central place in the ongoing education and activity of liberal arts scholars. The problem I am highlighting concerns its extension into undergraduate liberal education.

o o o

The prestige and authority of science—which helps explain the precariousness of general education in the modern university— also accounts for Freud's insistence on the scientific legitimacy of psychoanalysis. He presented his observations as "discoveries" and fought a skeptical medical establishment tooth and nail over their scientific validity. Freud was determined to claim the same authority he had presumed in his laboratory work for the bizarre ideas he developed about the mind. His quest for scientific respectability drives much of his psychoanalytic writing.

But the scientific straitjacket into which Freud tried to fit psychoanalysis never fit well. In retrospect, Freud's focus on clinical results and medical respectability looks like an artificial and probably counterproductive limitation. Psychoanalysis proposed a novel way of understanding what it means to live as a conscious human being. What it has to say about the nature of the mind has implications for every aspect of experience. It is only incidentally related to pathology. Psychoanalysis, in its broadest conception, treads the same grounds as liberal education inasmuch as both are concerned with the nature of human flourishing.

The effort to validate psychoanalysis through protocols of scientific demonstrability was bound to be unsatisfactory for the same reason that literary analysis cannot be reduced to a science. Both are modes of interpretation in which meaning emerges from the ambiguous margins—from allusions, symbols, resonances, subjective associations, patterns of sound, and patterns of sense. Interpretation in both literature and psychoanalysis is a subjective effort to reach a satisfying understanding. The form of knowledge generated by psychoanalytic interpretation is always situated in a particular subjective experience of the world. It is not generalizable or reproducible; it is always provisional and incomplete. The truths of psychoanalytic and

literary interpretation are pragmatic in the sense that William
James explained in his 1906 lectures on pragmatism: *"Ideas ...
become true just in so far as they help us to get into satisfactory relations with other parts of our experience."*[11]

The self-knowledge that results from psychoanalysis is not a
cognitive acquisition but an inward unfolding. In this, it resem-
bles the knowledge that results from a liberal education—a sort
of knowledge that ultimately resolves to a clearer view of oneself. In liberal learning, as in psychoanalysis, the act of knowing
transforms us. In knowing something about ourselves, we become something else; the thing that we know is changed by our
knowing it. The meaning and value of liberal education—and
of psychoanalytic insight—is always located in a specific life
and involves its subjective capacity for self-reflection. Jonathan
Lear gets at this similarity when he defines psychoanalysis
simply as *"facilitating the development of self-conscious thought*
in the analysand."[12]

o o o

My intellectual relationship with Freud—based on reading his
voluminous writings and teaching selected parts—is hard to
separate from my personal experience of psychoanalysis. And
the process of reflection and self-exploration in which I engaged through psychoanalysis is, again, hard to separate from
the broader impact of liberal education on my life.

---

11. William James, *Pragmatism* (Indianapolis and Cambridge: Hackett Publishing
Company, 1981), p. 30; the emphasis is in the original. While pragmatism as a philosophical system claims that this is actually the same notion of truth we find in the
sciences, many scientists disagree.

12. Jonathan Lear, *Freud*, 2nd ed. (New York: Routledge, 2015), p. 5; emphasis in
the original.

The summer after sophomore year at Columbia, I rented an apartment and got married. I never returned to living on campus. I joined the rush-hour commuters on the New York City subway system every morning, attended classes, worked my work-study job whenever I was not in class, and returned home to Queens in the evening. My experiment as a residential college student was over.

I had first met Michele when I was a junior in high school, and she was one of my brother's classmates at Queens College. She treated me like a pet, and I enjoyed her sisterly attention. When we reconnected the summer after my freshman year of college—when I was back home, sharing a room with Mom and Ray and living out of that old suitcase—it was a whole different story. Sparks flew everywhere. She was older, she was American (in the Puerto Rican sense), she was smart, she was pretty, she was emotionally intense, she was in love with me. My enormous hunger for intimacy had found a match.

We rented a tiny one-bedroom apartment in Sunnyside, Queens. Our life together was a shelter where I got love and companionship, and from which I made daily forays into the world I was trying to make my own. Building a home with Michele helped bring order to a world that came at me faster than I could assimilate and from unknown directions. It was a respite from upheaval. We had a cat. Then two cats. We had a car. We started going to church—Michele with the fervor of a new convert, and I with the been-there-done-that reserve of an old hand. I enjoyed the safety of known turf, but felt none of the ardor and devotion of my teenage years.

Not long after we moved in together, under the influence of her newly awakened faith, Michele proposed that we stop living in sin and either get married or separate. I thought about it for a few days, but it was not a hard decision. The sin was of no concern to me, but separating was unimaginable.

On a sweltering July afternoon that summer—against the advice of everyone we had consulted—Michele's brother Mike walked her from our bedroom to the living room, where my old pastor Ernesto Cervantes performed the wedding before a handful of friends and relatives. Mr. Philippides signed as the witness on my side; Michele's mother was the witness on hers.

A decade later, the uncoiling of my personality in psychoanalysis precipitated the unraveling of that marriage. Analysis was not the only factor, of course. Michele had reached a fork in her own road. We had moved back to Manhattan after three years in Queens, she had gone to Columbia for a master's degree, I was finishing a PhD in English, she was a teacher in a private school on the East Side. We drank martinis, I smoked pot, our closest friends were two gay couples who worked with Michele. At every turn, our cosmopolitan lives had become increasingly incompatible with the evangelical faith to which Michele felt called. Forces larger than we could contain drew us toward different worlds. We could not walk together into a shared future. After eleven years, we parted ways on amicable and even loving terms, but with the pain and heartbreak of the end of a world.

Physicists say that immediately after the Big Bang, the universe underwent a period of "cosmic inflation"—a short burst of astonishing expansion in which it assumed its fundamental features. Something like this happened to me in graduate school. It was the first time since arriving in the United States that my world had stopped spinning. In the relative stability of a PhD program, a campus job as a pre-med advisor, and my married life, a stable center began to form inside me, like the still eye of a hurricane. With this came a monster appetite for knowledge and newness. The intellectual tools I had developed as an undergraduate I now unleashed with fury on everything that crossed my path. I was the proverbial kid in the candy store. I took deep dives into classic jazz, Noam Chomsky, linguistics, the Metropolitan Museum of Art, Dominican politics, the *Economist*. I formed intense and fleeting friendships, explored New York City on foot, re-established contact with my father. My ardent diversions slowed down progress on the PhD, but I didn't care. What I was doing felt different than what my graduate school peers or even my professors were doing. In that period, my life assumed the dimensions it continues to inhabit.

o o o

I entered the PhD program in the Department of English and Comparative Literature at Columbia in the fall of 1995, immediately after graduating from college. After spinning my wheels for a few years, I chose early American literature and culture as my field of specialization. By the summer of 2002, I had passed my doctoral exams and was settling into a dissertation on anti-slavery and the American transcendentalists. As I had done since freshman year of college, I was working twenty hours a week in the School of General Studies' Postbaccalaureate Pre-medical Program. In June, I began psychoanalysis.

I had started seeing Phillip, my therapist, that spring. The ostensible motive was to get my little brother Ray to try therapy himself. He was fourteen then, disaffected from school, and finding it hard to sort out his complicated life. For three years, he had been living with Michele and me while attending Manhattan Country School, the progressive private school where Michele taught Spanish. On the recommendation of the school psychologist, I convinced Ray to join me in trying out therapy, seeing different therapists in the same practice and coordinating our appointments so that we would go there together. Our agreement was that if, after a few sessions, he didn't want to continue, he could stop. He did and I didn't.

After a few months, Phillip suggested that we shift from once-a-week therapy to Freud's signature modality: psychoanalysis. Much of the difference between the two comes from their intensity—psychoanalysis demands four or five sessions a week. The practice today is confined to a small corner of clinical psychology strongly concentrated on the island of Manhattan and a handful of other world cities. Because of the number of sessions involved each week and the corresponding cost of the affair, the practice requires abundant money as well as abundant leisure. If not exactly leisure, writing a dissertation gave me a lot of scheduling flexibility. So when Phillip proposed that we switch to psychoanalysis for the same reduced fee I was paying for therapy, I saw what an improbable and anomalous thing it was for someone like me to have the chance to pursue this esoteric program of self-examination, and I said yes.

In the early days, insights came fast. I was reading Ralph Waldo Emerson's journal. I was dreaming a lot. I was discovering the scent of a person whose track I had lost somewhere between Cambita and New York. I was individuating from Michele. I was allowing myself to breathe. I was unclenching my fists.

Phillip said to me one day, speaking (weirdly) in the first person, as if lending me his voice to say something I could not say myself: "The one thing I can't allow myself is to need anything from anyone."

On another day, I read in Emerson's journal that "Captain Franklin after 6 weeks traveling to the N. Pole on the ice found himself 200 miles south of the spot he set out from; the ice had floated."[13] I felt the ice on which I walked was floating, though I could not tell the direction.

I started writing down my dreams. I have them a lot. Phillip said one day that I was lucky to dream as I do. I had classic dreams: finding myself naked in public; performing in a play without knowing the script; unable to find the classroom where my class is meeting, for which I am also late. I also had a repertoire of recurring dreams that always returned with subtle variations, like jazz renditions of standard tunes: climbing, by hand, the complex latticework of the 59th Street Bridge, always terrified, and always going from Queens to Manhattan; finding myself in my grandma's house in Cambita, sad and searching for something I could not find; witnessing the apocalyptic end of the world at dawn from my father's porch, often perched on his shoulders.

I started to become aware of a dead space that lay between me and the world, between me and my own experience of myself.

I realized that I had not felt anger in years; I would not allow it. Gradually, I began to feel the emotion again. In dreams, it would sometimes break out like a tornado, devouring everything in its path. One night, I dreamed I was yelling at my father with all of my might, engulfed in an all-consuming rage. In the dream, I was yelling in English. I had never used the wrong language in a dream before.

One night, I dreamed of a disturbance beneath the floorboards in the first-floor apartment in Washington Heights where Michele and I lived. I went down to the laundry room in the basement to investigate the source and discovered a small mound of earth about the height of my chest. It was the tip of a

13. Ralph Waldo Emerson, *Journals and Miscellaneous Notebooks*, Merton M. Sealts Jr., ed. (Cambridge: Belknap Press of Harvard University Press, 1965), Vol. 5, p. 25 (March 27, 1835).

massive volcano growing under my apartment, irrepressible, spewing fumes and flames and making the ground shake. In the dream, as I see the mound, I understand that no one can escape, that it is going to consume the whole world.

o o o

Freud identified free association as the "fundamental rule" of psychoanalysis. His basic instruction to the patient was "say whatever comes to your mind." An invitation to free-associate is a pretty tricky request. In my own analysis, nothing was more certain to instantaneously erase every thought from my mind than Phillip asking me to tell him what I was thinking. The suggestion would produce a sort of affective paralysis. It made me dumb and mute. No words, no thoughts, just an oppressive awkwardness. It never lasted long, but it had a sickening intensity. After a few seconds, I'd move on to an agitated inner dialogue that was always some version of: "What should I say? What would Phillip like me to say? What is the most psychoanalytically sophisticated thing I can say?" My thinking seemed always trapped in a hall of mirrors.

The first lesson of free association is that it is never free. Precisely because free association pretends to be "unmotivated," it presents a canvas on which you cannot help but paint a true picture of yourself. When you free-associate, you make an effort—at which you always fail—not to censor anything that passes through your mind, as if, in Freud's words, "you were a traveller sitting next to the window of a railway carriage and describing to someone inside the carriage the changing view which you see outside."[14] Your task is to put aside any criterion

---

14. "On Beginning the Treatment," *Standard Edition*, Vol. 12, pp. 134–135.

of selection and not concern yourself with being proper, or interesting, or incisive, or impressive, or relevant. The analyst's job is to listen to this discourse in a special way, one that aims to capture from the flow of associations something that the patient does not know he or she is saying. In his 1912 paper "Recommendations to Physicians Practicing Psycho-Analysis," Freud called this special way of listening "evenly suspended attention," and described it as consisting "simply in not directing one's notice to anything in particular" and of "giving equal notice to everything."[15]

Phillip would often start sessions by asking me, "Where are you today?" More often than not, I could not come up with an answer. I could not get a fix on myself. Psychoanalysis confronted me with places unseen and unsuspected around which I had fashioned an asphyxiating stability. Like dark matter in the universe, which cannot be observed directly but can be detected because of its gravitational effects on objects around it, these dead spaces distorted my experiences and perceptions, suffused my life with a sense of hollowness and desperation. Starting psychoanalysis, I did not know, and could not suspect, that my peculiar psychic malaise, while permitting me a high degree of functionality by almost any measure, made it impossible for me to access an authentic sense of myself. It also made it impossible to make true contact with anyone else.

My life had been full of discontinuities, vast stretches of experience and emotion that existed like islands, incommunicado. I did not have the tools—the threads and the needles—with which to stitch together the patches that made up my life. I

15. "Recommendations to Physicians Practicing Psycho-Analysis," *Standard Edition*, Vol. 12, pp. 110–111.

possessed no language with which they could speak to each other. Analysis would mean working out terms of self-understanding capacious enough to assimilate the disparate lives that, nearing thirty, I had already lived. It would mean integrating parts of myself that were alien to one other and to achieve some sort of wholeness. In the strenuous effort that analysis required, I was motivated by a profound longing to live just one life.

Around this time, I saw Woody Allen's mockumentary film *Zelig* (1983). It wasn't funny that first time. It was just disturbing. Woody Allen's character, Zelig, is known as the human chameleon, a man without a center, without self-identity. His desperate need to be liked and accepted has caused him, without his knowing and without his being able to help it, to take on the characteristics of the personalities around him. In Zelig, I saw why I had such a hard time free-associating: it was almost impossible for me to access a sense of self except as a tool to ingratiate myself to others.

This is why at first I had resisted lying on the couch. As we were preparing to go from once-weekly sessions to the psychoanalytic standard of four sessions a week, Phillip left it up to me whether I'd lie on the couch (with him out of view) or sit on a chair facing him, as I had been doing in our therapy sessions. Explaining the reasons I didn't want to lie on the couch convinced me that I should do it. My hesitation boiled down to a need to monitor Phillip's reactions to what I was saying as I was saying it. I wanted cues about what would be the right things to say, the things he would want me to say, the things that would make me his favorite patient. Even before the analysis proper had started, I had bumped into something important: a dread of finding myself unmoored and an inability to relate to others except as an effort to win over their affection.

One day, Phillip blurted out, as if unable to help it, "Your damn charm is going to kill you!"

o o o

Five Lectures on Psycho-Analysis

The methods and insights that Freud worked out in psycho-analysis have been important in my ongoing process of self-understanding; they are essential tools in my continuing liberal education. Many of Freud's ideas were anticipated in literature and in philosophy well before his time, and he drew freely on ancient sources to sharpen his own intuitions. But he is unique for the systematic approach he developed, the brilliance of his exposition, and his effectiveness in popularizing his theories. It was this mission of exposition and popularization that brought him to America in 1909 to deliver his *Five Lectures on Psycho-Analysis.*

Freud delivered the *Five Lectures* at Clark University in Worcester, Massachusetts, on the occasion of accepting an honorary degree from its President, G. Stanley Hall. President Hall had invited leading American scientists and intellectuals to attend the lecture series as a way of introducing the young science of psychoanalysis to the country's intelligentsia. Present at the lectures were notable figures like William James, Franz Boas, and the political radical Emma Goldman.

Freud published two subsequent sets of lectures on psycho-analysis: the *Introductory Lectures to Psycho-Analysis* (1917), and the *New Introductory Lectures to Psycho-Analysis* (1932). Because of their concision and clarity, the 1910 Clark Lectures offer the most accessible overview of the major concepts in psychoanalysis. As texts, they stand somewhere between philosophical speculations, scientific expositions, and literary creations. They brim with suggestiveness, perspicacity, and charm. But what makes them most valuable for liberal education is the clear articulation of a set of concepts and practices that can inspire any reader to novel forms of self-analysis. Among these concepts and practices are: hysteria, or thinking with your body; listening to the unconscious; and the interpretation of dreams.

Hysteria, or Thinking with Your Body

Freud started his lecture series by giving credit for the origin of psychoanalysis to Joseph Breuer and his treatment of patient zero: Anna O. The breakthrough in the case was the "momentous discovery" that Anna's physical symptoms were not "capricious or enigmatic products of the neurosis" but, in fact, "residues—'precipitates' they might be called—of emotional experiences" from her past.[16] With his gift for epigrams, Freud boiled it down to a memorable bon mot: "*hysterical patients suffer from reminiscences.*"[17] As these memories were brought to consciousness under hypnosis, Anna experienced the strong emotions that she had suppressed during the actual events, and this "catharsis" brought relief from her debilitating symptoms. Freud understood that Anna was experiencing with her body what her mind refused to acknowledge.

Phillip said to me once that you can think with your body. Many of us experience this in the way we handle stress. One memorable example for me occurred in May 1999 and disrupted a particularly frantic period in my life. That winter and spring, I had been preparing for the oral exams in my PhD

---

16. *Standard Edition*, Vol. 11, p. 13.

17. *Standard Edition*, Vol. 11, p. 15; the emphasis is in the original.

program. I also had my campus job advising postbaccalaureate premedical students, working twenty hours a week during the semester and full-time during breaks.

This was also the third year of a program I had started that taught English to immigrants living in Washington Heights. I had set it up with two people from the Manhattan office of the Partido de la Liberación Dominicana, a then left-wing minority party that had, improbably, come to power in the Dominican Republic in 1996. Frank and Clodomiro, who became dear friends, would find the students and a venue; I would create a curriculum, teach the class, and, if necessary, hire and train other teachers.

I consulted various people at Columbia—experts in the teaching of English as a Second Language and people with experience administering academic programs—and they uniformly and somewhat condescendingly explained to me that what I was trying to do was much harder than I realized, that I should at least hire a consultant to help me. Ha ha ha. A consultant. It seemed to me that they didn't understand what I was doing. They thought that I was setting up a business. I ignored their advice, hired two other teachers, and started offering elementary and intermediate English to about sixty students. Most of them were Dominican, many of them taxi drivers, and some had only rudimentary literacy even in Spanish. We met on Mondays and Wednesdays from 6:00 to 9:00 p.m. I adapted an off-the-shelf English as a Second Language curriculum for the program, taught the elementary level, and helped organize the fundraisers (raffles, parties, etc.) that, each month, achieved the miracle of bringing in enough money to pay the other teachers.

Ah, youth. It was a crazy thing to do, really. But that didn't matter; even if the program succeeded only a little, it would have still been worth doing. Teaching English to immigrants who were struggling to get by in New York was, literally, giving them a voice with which to participate in the broader world around them. And with six hours a week, you could really get somewhere. Every week, they could say new things and do new things. Before class and during breaks, they would regale each other with stories of the new feats of communication they had attained: giving directions, understanding an announcement by the train conductor, deciphering a news headline, telling the doctor where it hurt.

This was during the time when Michele was studying applied linguistics at Columbia's Teacher's College, focusing on second-language acquisition. With what I absorbed from her and my own experience of learning English, I believe I made a competent teacher for my students. But the key ingredient was my identification with them and theirs with me. We fully recognized each other and quickly grew to love each other.

Taking a page from how Michele taught Spanish to middle school second-language learners, I didn't allow any Spanish in the classroom. This meant a lot of pantomime and a lot of drawing figures on the chalkboard, like a game of charades. We would play-act scenarios in the classroom—visiting the downtown office of the Immigration and Naturalization Service, applying for a job, ordering food at a restaurant, being stopped and frisked by the police. These skits generated the most hilarious turns of creativity and wit. We learned about Thanksgiving and the Electoral College, we sang songs from the American songbook, we parsed excerpts from State of the Union speeches. The thing that sustained the crazy experiment for the three years it lasted was the attachment and solidarity we all developed.

By that time, I had been living in the United States for thirteen years. Until I got to college and onto student health insurance, a meal plan, and a work-study job, my life looked very much like many of theirs, making ends meet with the help of food stamps, welfare, and section 8 housing assistance. What motivated me was an urge to pass on to them anything that my experience suggested would be useful as they made their own way in America. I wasn't just teaching them English, but trying to forge tools with which they could transform their reality. I was trying to restore a dimension of agency in their lives that had been lost in leaving their native culture. I wanted to introduce them to possibilities that were invisible from where they stood. I wanted to make intelligible to them the entire world I had come to live in.

It was the most meaningful kind of teaching I have ever done.

That same spring, I was also teaching a very different kind of course to a very different kind of student: the notoriously demanding (and now extinct) Logic and Rhetoric, the first-year composition requirement for Columbia College students. I had myself painfully learned the rudiments of expository writing in this class just a few years earlier. For the first half of the semester, students wrote two short papers each week, which I reviewed and corrected line by line. Later in the semester, they wrote one paper a week. As anyone who has taught first-year composition knows, the work is grueling. But that too was exhilarating. I was learning to teach students not just how to express their thoughts, but how to form them: how to think about the world around them clearly and incisively. On these students, too, I poured myself without reserve.

They were busy times. During the day, I advised postbac premed students on getting into medical school and wrote the comprehensive recommendation dossiers that accompanied their applications. Then I taught Columbia first-years how to write clearly and precisely. Then I traveled north two miles to a different world and taught Dominican adults about how to live in America.

About January of that year (1999), I scheduled my PhD oral exam for April 1. The exam would cover a reading list of 120 books in my three chosen fields: Orality and Literacy, American Puritans, and African-American Language and Literature. After finding my feet in that hectic spring semester, I organized a reading schedule and realized, with horror, just how much material I'd have to get through *every single day*, without breaks, to be ready for my April Fool's Day exam.

Every night I'd get home, close to 10:00 p.m. on teaching nights, put on headphones, and listen to Billie Holliday while reading for a few hours. I'd then take off the headphones and put into notes the most important things I had encountered in the reading. Weekends were marathons of grading and reading for the exam.

Thursday, April 1, arrived, and I took my orals. At the end of the two hours, I stepped outside the seminar room in Philosophy Hall where I had been examined by four professors and waited as they deliberated on my performance. When I came back into the room, the chair of the examining committee told me that while the committee could not formally award a "pass with distinction," they all felt that I had given a distinguished performance on my exam. As we were leaving the room, the professor overseeing my subfield on American Puritans, and who would later become my dissertation advisor, joked that I could now take the weekend off. But I actually couldn't, since I had two classes to teach on Monday and a stack of papers to grade on the weekend.

It was around this time that I noticed a bald spot on the back of my head, right above the base of the skull and a little to the left. It was about the size of a quarter and growing. When I ran to the bathroom, held up a hand-mirror, and examined the horrid spot, a freezing chill ran down my spine. I probably had brain cancer. My visit to the Columbia Student Health Service the next morning did not confirm this suspicion. The nurse practitioner who saw me prescribed a cream and told me that sometimes this can happen as a response to stress. "Have you been stressed lately?" With full sincerity and seriousness, I said, "No, I haven't." And it was true. In a way. Throughout those months of resolute intensity, I did not *feel* stressed. I felt fine. I did not even feel particularly tired. If anything, I felt energized.

No, I had not felt stress from the combined demands of my job as a premed advisor, my college teaching, running the ESL program, and my orals preparation. Instead, I grew a bald spot on the back of my head. And in case the message my body was sending wasn't clear, six weeks after my orals, while playing softball, I ran fast to slide into second base and, with one cracking misstep, broke my right tibia and fibula. I did it without intervention from anyone, all through my own effort.

My leg and my bald spot both recovered over a summer spent almost entirely sitting on a couch and looking out the window.

My bald spot was simply a stress-induced physical ailment. Those are common and widely recognized. What makes it psychoanalytically significant is that I was completely unconscious of the stress. In sealing myself off from it—in not allowing myself to feel my own reality—I was enacting a central defensive mechanism I'd used throughout my life and which in this case gave a dramatic sign of its inadequacy and its danger. In my failure to allow myself a conscious experience of what I was feeling, I was displaying the underlying symptom Freud came to recognize in all neuroses: a denial of reality.

My self-inflicted leg break is even more illustrative of what Freud began to see in his treatment of hysteria. I broke my leg because I was running too fast on that Saturday morning. A few weeks later, I returned to the field wearing my cast to show everyone I was OK. Which, of course, I wasn't: my leg was broken in two places, and I was on crutches. On the day of the accident, while I sat on second base waiting for the ambulance to arrive, my back had grown tired, and the ever-kind Barbara Hanning sat back-to-back against me so I could rest. Overjoyed at seeing me now, Barbara reassured me that I would return to the game before long, adding, "But you will probably not run bases with the same bravado."

I had not realized that I ran bases "with bravado." But it was true. I ran with breakneck abandon. The particular moment of the accident had a fractal relation to my entire life: the softball field was not the only place where I was running too fast and with a kind of frenzy that I could not sustain or control. I broke my leg and forced myself to sit down for three months. The injury I had inflicted on myself seemed to have a symbolic relation to an unconscious situation I was living. As if unable to reason out that I needed to slow down, my body brought it about through other means.

The Unconscious Speaks

Self-deception is a pervasive feature of human life. We are almost constantly engaged in it in one way or another. Self-deception is a manifestation of the unconscious at work—one part of our mind is lying to another, and "we" are not aware of it happening.

The treatment of hysteria using hypnosis revealed to Freud that patients suffered from traumatic memories that had been split off from consciousness. The fact that these memories were not truly lost but kept in some separate part of the mind led him to posit a force that kept them there and prevented their admission into consciousness. He called this force *resistance* and the process by which this force bars problematic memories from consciousness *repression*:[18]

> Perhaps I may give you a more vivid picture of repression and of its necessary relation to resistance, by a rough analogy derived from our actual situation at the present moment. Let us suppose that in this lecture-room and among this audience, whose exemplary quiet and attentiveness I cannot sufficiently commend, there is nevertheless someone who is causing a disturbance and whose ill-mannered laughter, chattering and shuffling with his feet are distracting my attention from my task. I have to announce that I cannot proceed with my lecture; and thereupon three or four of you who are strong men stand up and, after a short struggle, put the interrupter outside the door. So now he is "repressed," and I can continue my lecture. But in order that the interruption shall not be repeated, in case the individual who has been expelled should try to enter the room once more, the gentlemen who have put my will into effect place their chairs up against the door and thus establish a "resistance" after the repression has been accomplished. If you will now translate the two localities concerned into psychical terms as the "conscious" and the "unconscious," you will have before you a fairly good picture of the process of repression.[19]

Freud does not see repression itself as problematic. Indeed, as he would drive home in what is probably his most widely read book, *Civilization and Its Discontents*, repression is absolutely essential for civilization. The problem with hysterics is not that they have repressed something, but that their repression has

---

18. *Standard Edition*, Vol. 11, pp. 22–23.
19. *Standard Edition*, Vol. 11, p. 24.

been ineffective. To explain this, Freud returns to the example of the unruly person who has been expelled from his lecture:

> If you come to think of it, the removal of the interrupter and the posting of the guardians at the door may not mean the end of the story. It may very well be that the individual who has been expelled, and who has now become embittered and reckless, will cause us further trouble. It is true that he is no longer among us; we are free from his presence, from his insulting laughter and his *sotto voce* comments. But in some respects, nevertheless, the repression has been unsuccessful; for now he is making an intolerable exhibition of himself outside the room, and his shouting and banging on the door with his fists interfere with my lecture even more than his bad behaviour did before. In these circumstances we could not fail to be delighted if our respected president, Dr. Stanley Hall, should be willing to assume the role of mediator and peacemaker. He would have a talk with the unruly person outside and would then come to us with a request that he should be re-admitted after all: he himself would guarantee that the man would now behave better. On Dr. Hall's authority we decide to lift the repression, and peace and quiet are restored. This presents what is really no bad picture of the physician's task in the psycho-analytic treatment of the neuroses.[20]

In the neurotic patient, the repressed memory continues to erupt into consciousness in the form of a hysterical symptom. In other words, hysterical symptoms are substitutes for the repressed material. Freud's entire psychoanalytic method hinges on the proposition that these substitutes—the symptoms—are not arbitrary ailments but bear an "indirect resemblance" to

---

20. *Standard Edition*, Vol. 11, pp. 25–26.

their repressed origins. At the opening of the fifth of the *Introductory Lectures*, he made the point with typical flair: "One day the discovery was made that the disease symptoms of certain nervous patients have a meaning."[21] Symptoms are not merely the *result* of unconscious thought patterns but their *expression*— the two are semantically linked. Like a word in a language, the symptom corresponds to a meaning. But whereas in natural languages the relationship of the word and its meaning is arbitrary, in psychic life the symptom is linked to its unconscious origin by an organic resemblance, like a shadow is related to the body from which it is cast or a protein is related to the segment of DNA from which it is transcribed. With neurosis, some psychic experience has proved impossible to integrate into the patient's sense of self and instead has been repressed from consciousness. But the repression leaks, and the leaks encode the unconscious material.

Freud and some of his followers sometimes spoke of the unconscious as if it were a separate and reasoning mind, obeying its own bizarre logic. But I find it easier to think of the unconscious as the repository of a form of psychic conditioning, as a kind of root programming that shapes how our conscious mind works in ways that escape our notice. For Freud, the unconscious contains the basic configuration of the instinctual drives that power our psyche. The most basic layer of this organization is established in early childhood, typically in response to the dynamics of our nuclear family; ultimately, it underlies our personality. Like the eyes in our head, this root programming is invisible to us except as reflected in a mirror. We see *through* them, but cannot see *them*.

---

21. *Standard Edition*, Vol. 15, p. 82. In a footnote, Freud explains that the discovery was by Joseph Breuer in the years 1880–1882.

Psychoanalysis concerns itself with bringing some of this underlying psychic conditioning into conscious awareness. Its promise is that the progressive elucidation of these unconscious structures can deepen the experience of our own lives and give us some degree of freedom from the compulsions they impose. We live in a cage whose dimensions are set by an unconscious order established in early life. Psychoanalysis is a method of expanding the floor of that cage.[22] To the extent that psychoanalysis—and, in fact, any form of introspection—uncovers aspects of our experience that were previously invisible and unsuspected, it enriches our lives and creates new possibilities for living authentically.

As Freud came to see in his mature clinical practice, the job of the analyst is not simply to uncover a patient's unconscious, but to facilitate a process that has been, for some reason, strangled, so that the patient can incorporate previously unconscious material into a fuller sense of him or herself. As psychoanalysis has expanded away from the debilitating forms of neurosis that Freud treated and into more ordinary kinds of psychic distress, this idea has been refined further, with an emphasis on the unconscious not as something that needs to be revealed, but as something that needs to be *experienced* by the patient in a conscious way. Unconscious material doesn't require exposure but translation. We can think of the unconscious not as something that needs to be disclosed but as something that needs to be ripened and integrated into consciousness. Psychoanalytic insight is not an add-on to the self but a metamorphosis of the self—it's the realization of the caterpillar that it has been living in a cocoon and the discovery, upon emerging, that it is actually a butterfly.

---

22. I owe this arresting image to Noam Chomsky's discussion of a slogan used by labor organizers in Brazil. Noam Chomsky, interviewed by David Barsamian, "Expanding the Floor of the Cage," *Z Magazine* (April 1997).

Living with an awareness of the unconscious—that is, living alert to the clues and language of unconsciousness—re-orients our relationship to ourselves. It adds an element of humility to our self-certainties and opens vast possibilities for development, growth, and transformation. By making the unconscious element of human experience a direct object of investigation, Freud shone a light on a concealed dimension of Socrates's dictum that the unexamined life is not worth living.

Dreams

Psychoanalysis takes to heart the ancient, popular, and intellectually suspect idea that dreams have hidden meanings. The seriousness with which it takes dream interpretation is perhaps its most distinctive characteristic. "If I am asked how one can become a psycho-analyst," Freud told his American audience in the third of the *Five Lectures,* "I reply, 'By studying one's own dreams.'"[23]

Dreaming is so ordinary that we can forget just how strange a phenomenon it is. As a general rule, when you dream, you are not aware that you are dreaming, but take the dream to be your reality.[24] But dreams can be so bizarre and so *unlike* reality that you wonder how it is that you don't realize immediately that you are dreaming.

In dreams, we accept fundamental incongruities in the fabric of reality as if they were entirely normal. If in the course of a regular day, I discover that I can fly by pedaling in the air, I should

---

23. *Standard Edition,* Vol. 11, p. 32.

24. The strange phenomenon of lucid dreaming—when you are aware that you are dreaming—is, of course, the exception to this general rule. But lucid dreaming is extremely rare.

realize immediately that I am dreaming; but I don't—I just go on thinking that this is the way things are now: I can fly. If I find that I am in a seminar room teaching a class but have forgotten to wear pants, I should realize that I am dreaming; but I don't—I simply believe that this is what has happened, and I try to deal with the situation as best I can. The fact that in dreams we so easily accept an absurd world suggests that our grip on reality is much more tenuous than we imagine.

Freud considered *The Interpretation of Dreams*, first published in 1900, to be his most important work. When he learned that the eminent psychologist and philosopher William James would only attend one of his Clark lectures, he dedicated that day to dreams and the psychoanalytic method of dream interpretation.

Given the value Freud placed on free association, and the difficulty patients have when trying to do it, it's no surprise that he would develop a keen interest in dreams and turn every tool of psychoanalytic interpretation in their direction. Dreams are the closest one can come to perfectly free associations. Along with "errors," like slips of the tongue and free association on the couch, dreams offer the third major psychoanalytic window into the unconscious—and it is a far bigger and more transparent window than the other two. Freud called dream interpretation "the royal road to knowledge of the unconscious."[25]

Freud understood dreams, like hysterical symptoms, as distorted expressions of underlying unconscious thoughts. He called the mechanism of distortion in a dream the "dream-work," and the unconscious wishes it distorts he called the "latent dream." The narrative we reconstruct after we wake up—which adds another layer of distortion—is the "manifest dream." The manifest dream is a doubly disguised substitute for

25. *Standard Edition*, Vol. 11, p. 32.

the latent dream thoughts that motivated it. The distorting forces are the ego's defenses. In the relaxed state of sleep, these defenses are compromised and permit the emergence of material that has been effectively suppressed during waking hours:

> You can convince yourself that there are such things as latent dream-thoughts and that the relation between them and the manifest content of the dream is really as I have described it, if you carry out an analysis of dreams, the technique of which is the same as that of psycho-analysis. You entirely disregard the apparent connections between the elements in the manifest dream and collect the ideas that occur to you in connection with each separate element of the dream by free association according to the psycho-analytic rule of procedure. From this material you arrive at the latent dream-thoughts, just as you arrived at the patient's hidden complexes from his associations to his symptoms.[26]

Psychoanalytic dream interpretation tries to reverse-engineer the latent thoughts by unwinding the distortions of the dream-work. If, as Freud believed, the human mind is highly associative, the branching associations stemming from the discrete elements of the manifest dream will eventually begin to coalesce around significant nodes. These associative convergences reveal the unconscious thoughts that motivated the dream and that appeared disguised in various ways. In other words, by free-associating around each of the elements of the dream, you can begin to get a feel for what the mind was thinking about while you slept.

Dreams were a particularly rich source of discovery in my own analysis. For a while, I kept a dream journal. Many of my

---

26. *Standard Edition*, Vol. 11, p. 34.

dreams were vivid and transparent. I dream a lot. Or better put, I remember dreams a lot. I would walk into a session with a new dream as if I had received an overnight letter with instructions for a psychic scavenger hunt. Most of the time nothing came of it. We would bat around ideas and associations, with me proposing multiple interpretations—never resting from the compulsion to try to place myself one step ahead of Phillip. Sometimes, parts of our conversation about dreams would return to me like a motif in a symphony, appearing again and again and gaining in significance and weight as time went on.

One day, for example, I dreamed that I was in a prison. It was an elaborate dream full of strange and bizarre twists. Our efforts didn't seem to yield much, but at one point Phillip said, "And you are a man who dearly loves prison." That comment startled me. It is quite the opposite. Nothing matters to me more than my freedom, my independence, my self-determination. I cannot stand being compelled or expected to do anything. But I could not shake the irritating idea that I am a man who loves prison. It kept coming back, sometimes in a session with Phillip, but more often in my own ruminations. The idea eventually ripened into an insight: that in order to assert a self-defining impulse toward freedom, I always find, or make for myself, prisons.

During my six years of analysis, I also reached a satisfying interpretation of a different sort of dream, a recurring dream. The dream would have me back in Cambita, going into my *abuela* ("grandmother") Milita's house, where I mainly lived from the time my parents divorced when I was five to the day I came to the US when I was twelve. After my parents' break-up, Mom returned to Grandma's house, and I went with her. Keysi stayed with Dad. After Mom left for the US, Abuela Milita looked after me with absolute devotion.

The dream was always set in the period after Abuela Milita suffered a stroke that left her bedridden. The last few times I saw her, on return trips to DR, her speech was too blurred and too strange to understand. The awkwardness I felt sitting by her bedside was unbearable. So my visits were short and perfunctory.

Without her vivacious presence and upkeep, the house where I had spent most of my childhood felt strange and ghostly. The front doors, which opened to the small living room, were no longer ever used. One walked along the house through a side path—*el callejón*—and then entered the house through the kitchen in the back.

The recurring dream consisted in my walking along this path to the back of the house and then finding my way to Abuela's room through the dark, empty house. While some of the content varied each time—and sometimes this scene came as part of a longer dream—the atmosphere at this juncture was always the same: an empty, lifeless house and a desolate sense of loss. One of the last times I had the dream, I wrote about it in my journal and made a comment that would begin the process of interpretation:

Struck vividly by how I didn't grieve Grandma's death; didn't feel it; nor her illness. It was as if a stranger had fallen ill and was dying, not the sweet, loving, devoted, indulging second mother, a woman who would give me everything, and do everything, whose favorite and special charge I was. How was this? How did that come about that I dissociated myself so thoroughly from the loss of her, the love of her, the death of her? How is it that she almost ceased to exist for me? That she largely ceased from mattering?

But that period remains in my dreams. Keeps returning, returning, returning at night.

Eventually, I did come to feel some of the grief over Abuela's death that I had not felt when she died during my sophomore year of college. When I heard of it then, it was as if I had been informed of the death of someone I vaguely knew, or as if I had been merely reminded that a person long dead was actually dead. But sometime after I made that journal entry, I went through a period of intense grief over Abuela. I was living alone at the time, deep in psychoanalysis, and constructing a new sense of myself after my divorce from Michele. The psychic upheaval and then liberation of the divorce probably opened me up to experience things I could not experience before. It was a bitter but satisfying grief. For some weeks, alone in my bachelor apartment on 142nd Street, I would break into uncontrollable weeping over Abuela and over the missed opportunities to be with her in those last years. It would come on me unexpectedly. Sometimes in the middle of a TV show, in the shower, when I walked into the apartment, halfway through a plate of rice and beans. Gradually, the grief subsided and, with it, the recurrence of the dream.

I don't know if this holds true of all recurring dreams, but in this case, my dream seemed to be an attempt to grapple with an emotional shock that remained undigested in my unconscious. It's like the mind was turning it over, trying to resolve it, or bring it to the surface, to the conscious mind, where it could be integrated into my waking life. Until that happened, the material remained unresolved and continued to break into my dreams when my resistance let its guard down.

The manner in which this dream paved the way for a release of grief is illustrative of the special kind of knowledge involved in dream interpretation. No one could have "interpreted" my dream to show me that it was about my inability to grieve Abuela's death. Telling me that I had repressed my grief would have done nothing. The interpretation was not something I needed to learn but something I needed to *experience*. I had known for years that there was something amiss about how I took Abuela's death, that I was unable to give myself over to an emotional experience of it. But I couldn't do anything about it; I was locked into a posture I could not release. What the dream, with its insistence, gave me was an entry point, a set of images, emotions, and responses over which I could linger and which I would eventually transform into an experience of the lost emotion.

As with everything else, Freud formulated precise rules and principles for dream interpretation. *The Interpretation of Dreams* is a detailed exposition of the technique. Neither my prison dream nor the dream about Abuela offer good examples of strictly Freudian interpretation. Interpreting them did not come about through an explicit exercise of free association around discrete elements, and neither unearthed some dark and unacceptable wish. But in each case, an examination of the dream revealed an unconscious condition whose unraveling was liberating. The dreams were, without question, meaningful expressions of my psyche with the potential of deepening my experience of myself. Ruminating on the dreams, turning them over in my mind, letting my mind wander under their suggestions, revealed important things to me. Not every dream holds important meanings, but many do, and learning to live alert to this aspect of our psychic experience can be enormously enriching.

o o o

The *Five Lectures* introduce a number of other psychoanalytic concepts whose exploration in the classroom, and in one's own life, can yield profound insights. They are also largely free of the glaring limitations that Freud's thought is well-known for—his

prejudiced views on women and their psychosexual development, his understanding of homosexuality as the result of ar-
rested sexual development, and the dogmatic certainty with
which he insisted on many dubious claims. As with all thinkers
from the past, our moral censure has to be applied with discrimination and historical awareness. "In what way are they
right?" is almost always a more productive and a more difficult
question than "In what way are they wrong?"

Many of the students I teach at Columbia come to Freud
already comfortable with psychotherapeutic and psychophar-
macological intervention as a way to respond to various forms
of mental distress. But there are many, like me when I arrived
at college, for whom any form of psychological treatment represents an embarrassing personal failure and a sign of character
weakness. I have seen many of these students' attitudes changed
by our reading and discussion of Freud. And, every few years, I
hear back from someone whose life has been impacted by an
insight whose seed was planted in one of our Freud discussions.

Much of what I have gotten out of psychoanalysis has
emerged in this way, long after the analysis ended. Analysis
taught me to look at myself in a certain askance way, to be at-
tentive to what happens on the edges of my consciousness, to
be less certain of myself, and more suspicious of reason, sense,
and sanity. You learn to try to stay always a little off balance, just
enough to perhaps glimpse at something your conscious mind
has been refusing to see. Not coincidentally, this way of looking
at yourself is also a powerful way to read literature and to approach human situations generally; it opens vital new avenues
of meaning and discovery.

My analysis did not end in a deliberate way, nor out any sense
of completeness or closure. It ended because I accepted an administrative position at Columbia College as Director of the

Center for the Core Curriculum and would no longer have the flexibility to sit for four sessions a week. Philip and I had begun the analysis at the William Alanson White Institute, and I paid only the nominal fee I could afford as a graduate student. After a while, we moved on to Phillip's private office, with the same fee structure. After completing my PhD and getting my first job—as a poorly paid postdoctoral fellow in the Core Curriculum—the fee went up just a little. I still carry a fair amount of guilt that, just at the point when I could begin paying something approximating Phillip's professional fee, I quit the analysis.

o o o

Psychoanalysis, occurring when it did in my life, was very much about restoring my capacity for emotional thinking, for processing emotions in a more conscious way. At a basic level, it was about accepting that my life had achieved enough stability, predictability, and safety that I could loosen my grip, that it was safe to feel emotions. There were big, ugly emotions to be felt from which I shrank. They were like things stuck in my throat that I could not bring myself to swallow—things about my early family life, about abandonment, about the trauma of immigration, about the trauma of poverty and alienation.

But the most immediate and most frightening issue I was facing during my analysis was that my marriage no longer worked. I could not face the fact that the only intimate relationship I had in the world, a relationship that had in so many ways been my stable center, was, in fact, fatally unstable and that the effort it took to keep it whole was slowly strangling me. That thought, that emotional truth, was too devastating to consider; I could not hold my gaze on it. Ultimately, it was the analytic relationship itself that created the space in which this reality could emerge into visibility. I did not see it at the time, but over the course of the analysis, I transferred my attachment from Michele to Phillip and formed a kind of alliance with him. He offered me an open and non-judgmental intimacy. He did not need me to be any particular way. He was at ease with my restlessness, my lust, my fantasies, my conflicts. With him, I did not need to protect my image. I did not need to protect him from me. From him I wrested permission to pull away from and eventually divorce Michele.

Phillip told me once that some people experience adolescence when they are teenagers, and some when they are in their thirties. I was twenty and Michele was twenty-five when we got married in our apartment in Queens. There was a desperate and volatile intensity to our closeness. We held on to each other like you would to a plank after a shipwreck. But by the time I was finishing my PhD and she was thriving as a teacher in a fancy private school, I think that we both felt we were approaching safe shores. They happened to exist on different continents. In the eleven years we were married, Michele had many times decided we should break up, but I could not bear it and would claw her back in desperation—as if my life depended on our being together. Then one day it began to dawn on me that even if we broke up, I would be fine. The next time she proposed we separate, I agreed. And I would not turn back. The time had come to experience adolescence.

CHAPTER 4

Truth Is God: Gandhi

I wish I could take credit for the inclusion of Mahatma Gandhi on the list of required texts for the Introduction to Contemporary Civilization course at Columbia. But as with most of the changes adopted every three years, Gandhi's incorporation came about as the result of a broad consensus among the faculty that built over time.

I had started teaching Gandhi in my section of Contemporary Civilization in 2008, using the little latitude allowed instructors to introduce readings that are not on the required list. I was not alone in doing this—Gandhi worked extremely well in the classroom. Many students found him among the most rewarding thinkers we examined. By the time a syllabus revision year came around in 2011, enough teachers had experimented with Gandhi or knew of someone who had that the review committee's proposal that he be added to the required list of authors faced no opposition.

My interest in Gandhi had been sparked by something I heard as a freshman from Susan Joerling, my boss at my work-study job. Susan was one of the few meaningful friendships I made that first year—all of them in the office of the Dean of Students at the School of General Studies, where I worked. She was also the first person I knew up close who claimed to be an atheist. Aware of my earnest concern with the issue, she told me that the closest she had ever come to believing in God was reading Gandhi's *Autobiography* when she was around my age. I didn't turn to Gandhi to stem the loss of faith I was undergoing as a freshman, but the notion that I should read the *Autobiography* stayed with me.

I got around to it in 2007. For about a year, I had been meditating every day and was trying to understand the impact that this little habit was having on my mind. By then, I had also been teaching Introduction to Contemporary Civilization in the West for several years. Gandhi appealed to me as a way to branch out of the "Western" political tradition. So I was drawn to him both as an intellectual project and as an extension of the inner exploration I had undertaken through meditation. For me, it usually goes like that.

My life experiences and my education have habituated me to reading and studying for personal development, and ultimately for self-knowledge. This tendency has worked against a certain kind of scholarly career by making it difficult to engage the kinds of specialized questions whose investigation yields original contributions to an academic field. I have never had a fixed sense of intellectual—and therefore professional—direction. Perhaps the disruptions and disorientations of my early life have made an academic no-man's land the most psychologically satisfactory position to inhabit. My profession, as far as I can tell, is amateurism.

Like Socrates had twenty years earlier, Gandhi captivated me. I had never encountered anyone so relentless, even reckless, in the pursuit of an ideal. The ideal he pursued is what he called "Truth." He sought it through "experiments" that often left him frail, malnourished, and isolated, but which cultivated in him an indomitable will. His all-consuming passion for spiritual attainment might count as a kind of insanity. Had he not lived so recently and had his life not been so thoroughly documented, no one would believe that a person like Gandhi had existed in real life.

Gandhi boasted of holding no secrets, of living in the open, fully exposed to the scrutiny of all. His mode of living—in communal ashrams and on the road—was essentially public. Moreover, with his incessant writing and speaking tours, he strained to make his inner life visible. If Augustine is the ancient writer whose psychology we know most intimately, Gandhi is the modern figure who most determinedly sought to lay his soul bare to the world. But the more you look, the more elusive he becomes. Who was Gandhi, really? What drove him? What were his ultimate motivations?

From the time he began public service in the mid-1890s as a representative of the Indian community in South Africa, Gandhi gave a consistent if sphinx-like answer to these questions. As he says in the opening to the *Autobiography*:

> What I want to achieve—what I have been striving and pining to achieve these thirty years—is self-realization, to see God face to face, to attain *Moksha*.[1] I live and move and have my being in pursuit of this goal. All that I do by way of speaking and writing, and all my ventures in the political field, are directed to this same end. But as I have all along believed that what is possible for one is possible for all, my experiments have not been conducted in the closet, but in the open, and I do not think that this fact detracts from their value.[2]

---

1. "Literally freedom from birth and death. The nearest English equivalent is salvation." (Footnote in the original).

2. Mohandas K. Gandhi, *Autobiography: The Story of My Experiments with Truth*, Mahadev Desai, trans. (New York: Dover Publications, 1983), p. viii.

You might be forgiven if your first impulse is to dismiss these lofty claims. But in the case of Gandhi, behind these words stands one of the best documented lives in human history. One recent biographer suggests that he is "the most written-about person of the last hundred years"[3]—with a good deal of the writing done by Gandhi himself. His *Collected Works* run to one hundred volumes. His expressive energy is rivaled only by that other famous celibate, Saint Augustine. Studying Gandhi, one is forced to recognize that, as far as anyone can tell, which is very far indeed, spiritual realization is the consuming passion and organizing principle of his life. And he went to every length, often to the verge of death, to attain it. To see God face-to-face. Not in the afterlife, but in this life.

A year after Gandhi's assassination in January 1948, George Orwell wrote a review of the *Autobiography*, which had been published thirty years earlier. Orwell opened the essay with a memorable point: "Saints should always be judged guilty until proven innocent," confessing, later in the essay, to "an aesthetic distaste" for the man.[4] Teaching Gandhi to undergraduates and talking about him to people in general, I have encountered this reflexive skepticism and distaste. Often, people's first response to Gandhi—even people who know little about his life and work—is to dispute his supposed saintliness.

But what's unique and captivating about Gandhi is precisely his saintliness and, specifically, the *worldliness* of his saintliness. He was a Mahatma, or Great Soul, but he was also that most

---

3. Joseph Lelyveld, *Great Soul: Mahatma Gandhi and His Struggle with India* (New York: Vintage Books, 2011), p. 21.

4. "Reflections on Gandhi," *The Orwell Reader: Fiction, Essays, and Reportage*, introduction by Richard H. Rovere (San Diego, New York, London: Harcourt, 1984), p. 328.

worldly of things, a lawyer; and two even wordlier things: a journalist and a politician. The modern world offers no parallel of someone attempting so socially engaged a form of saintliness. For this alone, to me, he is worth close attention.

Gandhi presents a sort of limit case for what the human impulse for moral perfection can achieve. If you are interested in the possibilities of development for a human life—in what is possible for the human will to achieve, and for a human being to become—Gandhi should be of interest. Through constant experimentation on himself, he fashioned a life of striking originality, depth, and consequence.

o o o

One of the noteworthy things about Gandhi is that he failed to achieve almost everything he set out to accomplish. His big campaigns—against untouchability, for Hindu-Muslim unity, for non-violence as a national creed, for the empowerment of women, for the adoption of the spinning wheel and homespun cloth, for the preservation of village life against urbanization— produced only mixed results, closer to failure than to success. Even independence, such as India obtained, was not the *swaraj* ("self-governance") Gandhi had sought. Yet in a deeper sense, Gandhi seems to have succeeded in changing something fundamental about the world in which we live.

Starting in his mid-thirties, Gandhi divested himself of all property and wealth, taking a vow of non-possession (*aparigraha*) and choosing to live, dress, travel, and eat like India's poorest millions. At thirty-six, long married and having fathered several children, he took the vow of celibacy (*brahmacharya*), not only abstaining from any form of sexual gratification for the rest of his life, but striving ceaselessly to rid himself of sexual desire itself. He adopted the strict practice of *ahimsa*, non-violence, not only toward human beings but toward all forms of life. He dedicated his political career to the cause of the poor and dispossessed. He underwent long prison terms, subjected himself to extreme deprivations, exerted himself to the verge of death several times in order to oppose flagrant injustices, and is reported to have died with words of forgiveness for his assassin on his lips.

But it's hard to accept saints. They rub us the wrong way. Perhaps saintliness in actual human form is intolerable because its existence would be an indictment of our own shortcomings. We can't stand saints. In fact, we tend to kill them.

o o o

Gandhi's *Autobiography* was written when much of the work for which he is famous still lay in the future. It was full of surprises for me. It stimulated my thinking in ways that continue to develop and to influence how I live. The *Autobiography* is not the story of the Mahatma, or the great movement for Indian independence, or even of the satyagraha campaign against discrimination of Indians in South Africa. Gandhi deliberately stops the narrative around 1921, the point when the Indian National Congress comes under his leadership and adopts his program of non-violent non-cooperation as a means of achieving self-rule. At that point, he says, his life became "so public that there is hardly anything about it that the people do not know."[5]

---

5. *Autobiography*, p. 453. Readers interested in the extraordinary dramas that attended the Mahatma's eventful life would do better reading one his many biographies or watching the 1982 epic film about his life, *Gandhi*, directed by Richard Attenborough and starring Ben Kingsley.

The *Autobiography* is primarily concerned with Gandhi's inner transformations before he was called Mahatma and with the "experiments" (many of them dietetic) that drove his development into the "Great Soul" the world would come to know. In it, he is disarmingly candid about his personal shortcomings, his almost pathological youthful shyness, and the setbacks he suffered in his first attempts to make his way in the world.

The account of his difficulties after arriving in London in 1888, at the age of eighteen, to study law, reminded me of my own experience and that of many of my relatives upon coming to the United States. Like Gandhi, we found ourselves dazed by newness, in culture shock, and ill-equipped to adapt. He had convinced his mother to allow him to study in London by taking three solemn vows of abstinence: from meat, from alcohol, and from women. Even so, he faced a prohibition from travel by the elders of his Modh Bania subcaste and had to accept what amounted to excommunication as the price of traveling to Europe. The three vows gave his life in England its basic structure. In time, along with others he would adopt later, these vows became the instruments through which he sought self-realization as well as his primary method for mobilizing masses of people.

Describing the moment in South Africa when he renounced sex altogether, even with his wife, he wrote in the *Autobiography*: "The importance of vows grew upon me more clearly than ever before. I realized that a vow, far from closing the door to real freedom, opened it."[6] This kind of reverse logic is vintage Gandhi. He comes to see the vow of celibacy not as constraint but as a liberation, enlarging his freedom of movement among people, and allowing him to concentrate his energies on public service. His vow of non-possession similarly liberates him from

---

6. *Autobiography*, pp. 180–181.

toiling for gain and removes the power of others, including the state, to coerce him by threatening his possessions.

The capacity to adopt a vow is itself the expression of a kind of purity of will. Cultivating that capacity was indispensable in pursuing self-realization. Writing to one of his nephews about the importance of vows, he explained that "only they can hope some time to see God who have nobly determined to bear witness to the truth that is in them even at the cost of life itself. Taking vows is not a sign of weakness but of strength. To do at any cost what one ought to do constitutes a vow. It becomes a bulwark of strength."[7]

In Gandhi's view, in order to "see God," to know Truth, one must be prepared to die in the effort. A vow is an explicit declaration of this intention. It's as if only by committing to a value that is higher than life itself does one meet the condition for a revelation of God. God enters a human life through the opening created by settling on terms with death. In this light, the idea that a long life of comfort and ease should be the ultimate goal for a human life is atheism—the denial of God.

Is there anything, I sometimes ask my students, for which you would be willing to die? I ask them because I ask this question of myself.

o o o

Gandhi encountered difficulties at every step of his English sojourn. On the trip there, being "innocent of the use of knives and forks" and lacking "the boldness to inquire which dishes on

---

7. *The Moral and Political Writings of Mahatma Gandhi*, Raghavan Iyer, ed., 3 vols. (Oxford: Clarendon Press, 1986), Vol. 2, p. 106.

the menu were free of meat,"[8] he survived on sweets and fruits he had brought from home, consuming them alone in his cabin.

On the day of his arrival, he was visited by Dr. P. J. Mehta, for whom he had a letter of introduction. Dr. Mehta was wearing a top hat, which Gandhi picked up, admiring its smoothness, but passed his hand over it "the wrong way, disturbing its fur." Gandhi recalls: "Dr. Mehta looked somewhat angrily at what I was doing and stopped me. . . . The incident was a warning for the future. This was my first lesson in European etiquette, into the details of which Dr. Mehta humorously initiated me. 'Do not touch other people's things,' he said. 'Do not ask questions as we usually do in India on first acquaintance; do not talk loudly; never address people as "sir" whilst speaking to them as we do in India,'" etc.[9]

Perhaps every immigrant has a stock of stories like this. There is simply so much you don't know, and it shows with every awkward gesture as well as in the blunders you commit about things that are common knowledge to everyone else. Sometimes these lacunae in cultural knowledge persist for years. In my case, for example, it was many years from my arrival to New York before I learned how to dress for winter. The basics of winter dressing were not part of the communal knowledge circulating in the Dominican community from which I drew my lessons.

Somehow I formed the notion that nothing would surpass a leather coat for warmth and comfort. After finding a used one at a Goodwill store, I suffered the consequences of this idea for several winters. Not until graduate school, for instance, did I discover the significance of wool. Up until then, I only knew it as an unbearably itchy fabric, and it was beyond the grasp of my Dominican imagination why anyone would dress in it. It took

---

8. *Autobiography*, p. 38.
9. *Autobiography*, p. 39.

me a long time to learn that a wool sweater over a cotton shirt changes everything. Later still, I discovered down coats. Then cashmere, which you can wear right against your skin for a feeling of being held in a warm embrace. Winters no longer felt like impossible impediments to a happy life.

In London, Gandhi was racked with homesickness. "I would continually think of my home country. My mother's love always haunted me. At night, the tears would stream down my cheeks, and home memories of all sorts made sleep out of the question."[10] His eagerness to return home was so strong that he embarked for India the very day after being credentialed as a lawyer, "pining to see my mother."

He arrived in Bombay in 1891 only to learn that his mother had been dead for some time. His relatives had withheld the information so as "to spare me the blow in a foreign land."[11]

This episode in the *Autobiography* is one of those scenes you encounter in a book that resonates so deeply in your own psyche that you can never forget it. Although I credit my father as the decisive influence in shaping my orientation to the world, it is my mother I have always been most attached to. They are both alive and in relative good health, but I identify intuitively with Gandhi's shock. Perhaps it's because I have some inkling of what it means to lose a parent. Both, actually. I lost my father when he refused to join my brother and me in immigrating to the US. But I took that in stride. Not so when I had lost my mother to America two years earlier. By the time we reunited, we were both different and living different lives. The thing that had been taken away from me at the height of an intensely formative relationship was never to be restored.

---

10. *Autobiography*, p. 40.
11. *Autobiography*, p. 75.

o o o

The saddest day of my life was February 5, 1983. I was nine years old. On that day, I took the forty-mile road trip from Cambita to the Las Americas International Airport to see Mom and Tía Sula off to the United States. It was the farthest I had ever traveled from home, the first time I saw an airplane in real life, and the first time I felt the kind of grief that makes it impossible to imagine how life can go on.

The weeks leading to her departure were rough for everyone. Mom had gotten the first boyfriend I ever knew about, Samuel. He drove a mini-bus between San Cristóbal and Cambita, was young, handsome, and much too cool. You can imagine it: my brother Keysi and I *hated* him. It was the worst thing that could happen on the eve of Mom's departure. But it was happening. It was a double blow. Close to D-day, Mom and I mended fences— my desperation for her love was too great to resist her advances. Her warmth and tenderness dissolved my jealousy, at least when Samuel wasn't around. But Keysi held fast. Even though he also came to the airport to drop Mom off, he wasn't speaking to her. Later, I came to understand that it's easier to part with someone you love when you're angry at them. Having reconciled with Mom, I did not have that layer of emotional protection.

A cloud of doom hung over my head in the days before her departure. The thought that after Saturday she would be gone—that we could not imagine nor make any plans for after that date— was unbearable. And saying goodbye at the airport was like dying of sadness. As Augustine said once, "My heart which was deeply attached was cut and wounded, and left a trail of blood."[12] No

---

12. Saint Augustine, *Confessions*, Henry Chadwick, trans. (Oxford and New York: Oxford University Press, 1998), p. 109.

heart breaks like the heart of a child. And while it's true that children have an extraordinary capacity to heal from heartbreak, they are also irrevocably changed by it.

My mother came to the US with her sister Sula and her brother, Leopoldo. Their green cards had been sponsored by my uncle Fidias, who had come to the US on a tourist visa in 1960s, married a Puerto Rican woman, and eventually become a US citizen. Tío Leopoldo was a famously savvy smooth-talker, a *tigre*, who had left Cambita long before I was born and had made his way as a car driver in the capital, Santo Domingo. Mom and Sula, on the other hand, were probably the most unlikely characters to undertake a migration from the backwoods of a developing country to a global metropolis. I am in awe of their daring. They came to the US with no education, no job, no English, and the street smarts of two Dominican *campesinas* who had grown up in the mountains. How did they find the audacity to leave Cambita and venture into the forbidding otherness of Nueva Yol? And it was February. To come from the balmy tropics to the bitter latitudes of the North American coast in February!

When it happened, I had no conception of what it must have taken to do this; I was merely heartbroken. The personal cost to Mom never crossed my mind. At the age of nine, and as close as we were, I had not yet begun to see her as a real person, with a life of her own. But I did understand why she, Sula, and Leopoldo had left—there was a plan. Immediately after arriving in the US, they would petition for their kids to join them under the provisions of the Family Reunification Act (the same immigration law that had allowed their brother to petition for them). They executed this plan without delay. It was a simple plan. There was no other purpose to their sacrifice.

○ ○ ○

This was the plan: to bring a bunch of kids to Nueva Yol and hope for the best. Don't knock it. It was the most precious gift they could give us. They left their children in the care of others, left their relatives, their friends, their homes, their culture, their roots, and, perhaps unknown to them, much of their personal agency. They gave it all up and faced the toil and uncertainty of Nueva Yol, so that we—their kids—would have a shot here. Any kind of shot. Heartbroken as I was to lose my mother, *this* I understood: I was going to be given a shot in New York. A shot at what, I didn't know, but I knew it was somehow worth almost everything to Mom and Sula.

I hear stories from Mom and Sula of those years in the US. Their first home was with Tío Fidias, in a small shotgun apartment in Jersey City, New Jersey. The sister-in-law did not take well to the arrival of the deer-in-the headlights sisters, who had suddenly occupied her house and who must have looked like an impossible burden to offload. How were *those two* ever going to find their way in Nueva Yol and leave the care of their brother?

The stories are usually told through peals of laughter that sometimes suddenly turn to tears. Mom and Sula have invented alter egos, two *comadres* (a mother and her child's godmother) who speak in a Dominican backwoods vernacular to recall their first experiences in *los países* (the United States). They whip up the funniest improv skits you have ever heard. They love to tell the story of when they ventured out to the grocery store to buy a few things with which to cook themselves a meal but ended up wandering the isles confused, looking at the shelves, unable to decide what to buy. They could not, for example, bring themselves to buy *a whole carton* of eggs when they only needed two. Eventually they gave up, defeated by the variety, super-sizes, and alien logic of a supermarket.

Once, in their misery, they decided to give up the plan and return to DR. Sula was going call her husband, El Men, and ask him to buy her a plane ticket. Mom, however, didn't have anyone she could get such money from, but decided that, behind Tío Fidia's back, she would beg in the streets until she had collected the necessary amount. When Tía Sula heard of her plan, she broke down in tears and hugged her, promising, "I will never leave you. We either go together, or we'll stay." They stayed.

Once, Tío Fidia took them to Manhattan to visit some friends. Manhattan! Washington Heights! A bodega on every block! Dominican Spanish in the streets! They were elated. One person spoke to another, and that person spoke to an acquaintance who knew somebody, and Mom and Sula found places to live—in the apartments of two sisters who lived one block apart and who would help them find jobs in Brooklyn's booming garment district. In the meantime, Mom and Sula would help the sisters with housework and childcare. One of the sisters, Quica, took Mom. Fifa, the other, took Sula.

And, sure enough, they found jobs before long (and together) in a towel factory earning the minimum wage of $3.35 an hour. But it felt like a lot of money to them, Mom and Sula always add. At the factory, they met a woman named Catalina whose daughter had a cousin who lived alone in an apartment in Manhattan. Mom and Sula were introduced to him— Santiago, a kindly man in his forties who drove a taxi and rented an apartment at 145th Street and Broadway. Things went well at first. Bound by the universal brotherhood of immigration, Santiago helped Mom and Sula find their way around and alerted the drug dealers who kept order in the block to look out for them. They, in turn, brought domesticity to the apartment, kept it clean and cooked enough for three.

Then winter came. There was no heat or gas in the building, and Santiago started making himself scarcer and scarcer. Mom and Sula cooked on a small electric stove. They would bathe in Quica or Fifa's place in Brooklyn after work and would come home to cook and to sleep wearing their coats, hats, and gloves. My mother recalls the exact date when a friend they had made—Valentina—visited them and discovered their situation. A quick internet search tells me that January 21, 1984, was a Saturday, and that it was the coldest day in New York City that year, with a high temperature of 19 degrees Fahrenheit and a low of 8. The final straw for Valentina was discovering that the water in the toilet bowl was frozen over. She said, "*No es posible.* I am not leaving you here. You pack whatever things you need and come with me; you will stay in my apartment."

Tough times.

And I in Cambita, oblivious, sending letters asking for roller skates.

In her quiet, humble, long-suffering way, my mother, full of love and self-deprecation, is my greatest hero.

o o o

The plan worked out alright. I'd like to think that her gamble paid off. I count the chance of becoming an American as among the greatest fortunes of my life. I doubt that there is any place on earth my mother could have taken me where I could construct a life as rich and broad as I have here, in the United States, in New York City. I cannot take lightly the opportunity Mom created for me of taking part in the collective self-governance of the most powerful nation in the world. A nation, as Lincoln put it, "dedicated to the proposition that all men are created equal," and that has enshrined its basic commitment to human freedom in a Bill of Rights. Never mind the failures of that nation to live up to those high ideals. They are still the ideals to which it is pledged, the ideals that I, too, pledged allegiance to in May 2000 when I took the oath of citizenship and registered to vote on that same day. The idea of America calls upon me to hold the nation accountable to those founding ideals, to denounce its failings to achieve them, and to struggle with all my might for their realization.

o o o

Mom's experiences as an immigrant, as well as my own, frame how I think of Gandhi's work organizing and representing poor and disenfranchised Indian laborers in South Africa. His burning political concern, both in South Africa and in India, was for what the Italian Marxist theorist Antonio Gramsci called "the subaltern"—the socially voiceless who have been excluded from the possibility of political agency. Gandhi came to understand his spiritual advancement as indissolubly linked with the fate of that stratum of society.

In closing the *Autobiography*, published serially between 1925 and 1929, he wrote:

> To see the universal and all-pervading Spirit of Truth face to face one must be able to love the meanest of creation as oneself. And a man who aspires after that cannot afford to keep out of any field of life. That is why my devotion to Truth has drawn me into the field of politics; and I can say without the slightest hesitation, and yet in all humility, that those who say that religion has nothing to do with politics do not know what religion means.[13]

The guiding political philosophy in Western democracies— liberalism—has from its inception sought to separate the public

---

13. *Autobiography*, p. 454.

sphere from religious influence, insisting on the separation of church and state. Gandhi would probably point out that this separation is superficial. What liberalism rejects in actuality is not religion but sectarianism, and it does so in the name of ethical commitments that Gandhi considered to be essentially religious.

Gandhi had an ecumenical conception of religion. He recognized the legitimacy of all organized religions and urged against proselytization, believing that all religious paths, when pursued with purity and sincerity, led to the same revelation of Truth. His concern was with the religious life, not with religious belief. Particular religions, such as Christianity, Islam, and his own Hinduism, are valuable because they connect people to ancient traditions, give them a shared sense of identity, and provide paths for the spiritual fulfillment humans naturally seek. In this sense, all religions are true and are legitimate pathways to God. But beyond particular faiths, Gandhi recognized a "religion which underlies all religions,"[14] and from which every faith draws its validity. "The soul of religions is one," he wrote, "but it is encased in a multitude of forms. The latter will persist to the end of time. Wise men will ignore the outward crust and see the same soul living under a variety of crusts."[15]

For Gandhi, this universal religion boiled down to two great practical principles: truth (*satya*) and non-violence (*ahimsa*). Of these, Gandhi subsumed non-violence under the all-pervasive principle of Truth, which in his view already contained the practice of non-violence. His notion of Truth was identical to his notion of God. "I often describe my religion as

14. Mohandas K. Gandhi, *Hind Swaraj and Other Writings*, Anthony Parel, ed. (Cambridge: Cambridge University Press, 1997), p. 43.

15. *Moral and Political Writings*, Vol. 1, p. 569; *Young India* (Sept. 25, 1924).

religion of Truth. Of late," he wrote in 1935, "instead of saying God is Truth I have been saying Truth is God . . . nothing so completely describes my God as Truth."[16]

In the Introduction to the *Autobiography*, he elaborates on his conception of truth:

> For me, Truth is the sovereign principle, which includes numerous other principles. This truth is not only truthfulness in word, but truthfulness in thought also, and not only the relative truth of our conception, but also the Absolute Truth, the Eternal Principle, that is God. . . . I worship God as Truth only. I have not yet found Him, but I am seeking after Him. I am prepared to sacrifice the things dearest to me in this quest. Even if the sacrifice demanded my own life, I hope I may be prepared to give it.[17]

Gandhi's commitment to truth is absolute. He seeks not only "truthfulness in word"—that is, never knowingly lying or misrepresenting the truth—but "truthfulness in thought also." For him, the search for truth required inner purification; it was one with the shedding of self-seeking and egotism.

Truth requires selflessness because you cannot see a thing for what it really is unless you can look at it without a personal agenda, without wanting anything from it. Any degree of self-interest acts as a distorting lens. The prerogatives of the self, in other words, are the fundamental impediment to seeing truth—not only in its absolute or transcendent sense, but in its relative commonplace sense. Gandhi therefore sought to starve the self of its ordinary sustenance through adherence to three lifelong vows: *brahmacharya* (celibacy, not only in action, but in thought), *aparigraha*

---

16. *Moral and Political Writings*, Vol. 1, 461.
17. *Autobiography*, p. ix.

(not only poverty, but non-possession), and *ahimsa* (non-violence, again, in action, speech, and thought). These commitments to purification in the pursuit of truth engendered subordinate resolutions, like frequent fasts, weekly days of silence, and the reduction of his diet to fruits, nuts, and, as a concession to the brute requirements of sustenance, goat's milk. "If you would swim in the bosom of the ocean of Truth," he declared in 1931, "you must reduce yourself to zero."[18]

Complete transcendence of the self—becoming "zero"—would constitute *moksha*: "The body exists because of our ego. The utter extinction of the body is *moksha*. He who has achieved such extinction of the ego becomes the very image of Truth."[19] Attaining this Truth was Gandhi's all-consuming determination.

Despite his extraordinary commitment, Gandhi was painfully conscious of his failures to live up to his ideal and repeatedly expressed disdain for the title of Mahatma. He insisted on his own inadequacy, but also on the resoluteness of his effort:

> I see truth every day clearer and clearer. The process through which the soul has been passing is an effort of the heart. The intellect has been hooked to its service by prayer, meditation, and constant watchfulness. . . . It has been an unfolding, drawing out or perhaps better still removing the hard and ugly crusts that overlay the truth that is within us. In other words, the process has been one of purification.[20]

When faced with struggles and setbacks, whether in the personal sphere, or on the large canvas of national politics, Gandhi's instinctive response was to intensify his *tapascharya*,

---

18. *Moral and Political Writings*, Vol. 2, p. 167.
19. *Moral and Political Writings*, Vol. 2, p. 194.
20. *Moral and Political Writings*, Vol. 2, p. 196.

or self-sacrifice, through fasts, penance, and ever wider renunciations. "Morally," he wrote in the *Autobiography*, "I have no doubt that all self-denial is good for the soul."[21]

Gandhi's resolve to subdue the self helps explain his passion for service. He saw service to the downtrodden—without attachment to results or the expectation of recognition—as a way of depriving the self of its primacy, opening the way for truth to shine forth through one's life, like a lens cleansed of grime. "The aim of man in his life is self-realization. The one and the only means of attaining this is to spend one's life in serving humanity in a true altruistic spirit and lose oneself in this and realize the oneness of life."[22]

○ ○ ○

Of truth, it can be said—as Augustine said of time—"I know exactly what it is provided no one asks me."[23] When Jesus told Pontius Pilate, who was presiding over his fate, that he had come to the world "to bear witness unto the truth," the world-weary Roman official asked him point-blank, "What is truth?" But Jesus didn't answer.[24]

Gandhi also demurred from giving a fixed definition of truth, declaring that "it is indescribable because it is God."[25] Nevertheless, a lot can be said of truth. Jesus, for example, said, "Ye shall know the truth, and the truth shall make you free."[26] This statement is striking in that Jesus does not say that *the truth* will

21. *Autobiography*, p. 292.

22. *Moral and Political Writings*, Vol. 2, p. 77.

23. *Confessions*, XI.xiv.17, p. 230.

24. John 18:37–38 (KJV).

25. *Moral and Political Writings*, Vol. 2, p. 156.

26. John 8:32 (KJV).

set you free, but that *knowing* the truth will *make* you free. In other words, the operation of truth is not that of an external force acting on you and giving you freedom, but of an inward realization that liberates you from within.

While he insisted on its elusiveness, Gandhi also said much that went beyond the tautology "Truth is God" to explain his deepening perception of truth as the fundamental law of existence: "Truth is That which Is, and Untruth is That which Is Not" ... "Laws of nature are expressions of Truth, and Virtues are forms of Truth";[27] and "The way to truth is paved with skeletons over which we dare to walk."[28] That last declaration, which constitutes the entirety of a letter written to his British devotee Mira Behn less than a year before his assassination, expresses something that Gandhi came to see with greater and greater clarity toward the end his life: the vitality, and even ruthlessness, involved in an uncompromising commitment to truth.

o o o

One of the reasons Gandhi preferred the formula "Truth is God" to "God is truth" is that "not even atheists have denied the power of Truth" and most have, in fact, rejected God precisely out of "their passion for discovering Truth."[29] "Denial of Truth," he concludes, "we have not known."[30] Gandhi recognizes that "truth" as a general concept is rather difficult to deny. To say that "there is no such thing as truth" is to say that "*what in fact is true* is that 'there is no such thing as truth.'"

---

27. *Moral and Political Writings*, Vol. 2, p. 151.
28. *Moral and Political Writings*, Vol. 2, p. 201.
29. *Moral and Political Writings*, Vol. 2, p. 165.
30. *Moral and Political Writings*, Vol. 1, p. 461.

But the "denial of Truth" that Gandhi claimed "we have not known" had already been launched by European philosophers decades before he made the statement. Friedrich Nietzsche, Satan's most acute theologian, is probably the key figure in the modern philosophical challenge to truth. He unleashed the intellectual current that today we associate with Postmodernism and Deconstruction and which questions the very category of truth. To use Martin Heidegger's formulation, "truth," like "being," is a concept that must be put "under erasure"—our language demands its use, but its use always involves a metaphysical sleight of hand.

Nietzsche saw no possibility of truths that exist independent of particular human interests—that is, truths that exist as objective entities graspable by pure intellect. He rejected the notion of "objectivity" to begin with, along with the idea of a "pure intellect" that can look at the world from a neutral vantage point, abstracted from its own positionality and interests. Instead of "truth" as conceived in the metaphysics of Plato and popularized through Christianity, for Nietzsche there are only perspectives, interpretations, and stakes: "For the human intellect," he wrote in his most sustained meditation on truth, "has no further tasks beyond human life."[31]

Nietzsche's brilliant escape from the circularity of an argument that claims that the actual truth is that there are no truths, is to challenge the concept of truth itself. He does not propose an alternative truth, but rejects the very category. Instead of wading into the metaphysical quicksands of transcendence, Nietzsche asks a more human set of questions: What role, what

---

31. Friedrich Nietzsche, "On Truth and Lie in a Nonmoral Sense" (1873), in *On Truth and Untruth: Selected Writings of Friedrich Nietzsche*, Taylor Carman, translator and editor (New York: Harper Perennial, 2010), p. 18.

function, does the category of truth serve? What function has it served in humanity's development? What interests does the notion of truth serve? Under what conditions did we invent the notion of truth, and what ends does it advance?

Nietzsche presents the notion of truth as a conceptual illusion, a trick of language, a human convention that satisfies specific social needs. We simply cannot stand apart from our peculiar psychology and anthropological constraints and see the world as it exists "in itself."[32] "What, then, is truth?" he asks in his 1873 essay "On Truth and Lie in a Nonmoral Sense": "A mobile army of metaphors, metonymies, anthropomorphisms—in short a sum of human relations that have been poetically and rhetorically intensified . . . truths are illusions of which one has forgotten that they are illusions."[33]

Nietzsche dispatches the idea of "objectivity" with a similar maneuver, not by proposing a "subjective" alternative, but by denying the entire category as "an absurdity and a nonsense," a "conceptual fiction" that demands "an eye turned in no particular direction." "There is *only* a perspective seeing," he insists in *On the Genealogy of Morals*, "*only* a perspective 'knowing.'"[34] The illusion of objectivity, however, is persistent in man, such that "it even requires some effort for him to admit to himself that an insect or a bird perceives a world utterly different from man's, and that it is senseless to ask which of the two perceptions of the world is correct, since that would have to be measured against a standard of *correct perception*, which is a nonexistent standard."[35]

---

32. *On Truth and Untruth*, pp. 15–49.

33. *On Truth and Untruth*, p. 30.

34. Friedrich Nietzsche, *On the Genealogy of Morals and Ecce Homo*, Walter Kaufmann, trans. (New York: Vintage Books, 1967, 1989), p. 119.

35. *On Truth and Untruth*, p. 36.

While offering a formidable challenge to the notion of truth as an unchanging metaphysical entity that can be grasped by the understanding, Nietzsche ultimately affirms the possibility of seeing through the "illusions of which one has forgotten that they are illusions." This is what his own philosophical project aims to achieve: a liberation from "the seduction of language (and of the fundamental errors of reason that are petrified in it)."[36]

On seeing that there are no metaphysical entities behind our illusions—that it is illusions all the way down—one arrives at the postmodern condition. In a famous passage in what is probably his most important book, *Of Grammatology*, Jacques Derrida declared, "*Il n'y a pas de hors-texte*," translated by Gayatri Spivak as both "there is nothing outside of the text" and, more literally, "there is no outside-text."[37] In other words, we live in a world of signifiers with no ultimate signifieds. Truth is interpretation, with no transcendent or metaphysical "there" there.

This unmooring of human reason from the possibility of ultimate truth in effect undermines all of Western metaphysics ("what is the nature of existence?"), including ethics ("how should I live?") and epistemology ("what can be known?"). All of these inquiries presume a bedrock reality that is available to the human intellect. To me, the destructive force of what Nietzsche unleashed warrants his extravagant claim: "I am no man. I am dynamite."[38] He subtitled his 1888 book, *Twilight of the Idols*, "How to Philosophize with a Hammer." In the retrospective evaluation of his own work that he offered in *Ecce Homo*, he explained that "what is called *idol* on the title page of the book

---

36. *On the Genealogy of Morals*, p. 45.

37. Jacques Derrida, *Of Grammatology*, Gayatri Chakravorty Spivak, trans. (Baltimore and London: Johns Hopkins University Press, 1974, 1976), p. 158.

38. *On the Genealogy of Morals*, p. 326.

is simply what has been called truth so far." His project in *Twi-light of the Idols*, indeed in his whole work, was to undermine the conceptual foundations of the Western philosophical edifice and thereby liberate the intellect into new and uncharted territory: "*I am he that brings these glad tidings,*" he said.[39]

Not surprisingly, Nietzsche's effort to pull the rug out from under the European philosophical tradition led him to examine the origins and function of morality—that system of norms and "truths" that claims for itself the extraordinary authority of regulating human behavior. The result was the 1887 *On the Ge-nealogy of Morals: A Polemic*, Nietzsche's most systematic and accessible presentation of his thought. He lays out his guiding question in the Preface: "Under what conditions did man devise these value judgments good and evil? *And what value do they themselves possess?*"[40] In the three loosely connected essays that follow, Nietzsche traces the emergence and evolution of moral concepts like good, evil, guilt, punishment, and self-denial, revealing them to be highly effective expressions of what he came to consider the fundamental principle of life: the will to power. As he would write in the concluding fragment of his unfinished *The Will to Power*: "Do you want a name for this world? A solution for all of its riddles? . . . This world is the will to power—and nothing besides! And you yourselves are also this will to power—and nothing besides!"[41]

Power, then, became Nietzsche's master concept. He understood the hierarchies established by judgments such as true and false, right and wrong, and good and evil as means of asserting

---

39. *On the Genealogy of Morals*, p. 314; the emphasis is in the original.

40. *On the Genealogy of Morals*, p. 17; emphasis in the original.

41. *The Will to Power*, Walter Kauffman and R. J. Hollingdale, trans. (New York: Vintage Books, 1967), sec. 1067, p. 550.

and maintaining specific configurations of power. "Every animal," he wrote in the *Genealogy*, "instinctively strives for an optimum of favorable conditions in which it can expend all of its strength and achieve its maximal feeling of power."[42] Even the characteristic asceticism of the seeker of truth, he argued, boils down to "a desire to rule over life."[43]

Among Nietzsche's intellectual descendants, Michel Foucault is the great theorist of power. Over the course of his tragically short but brilliant career, Foucault performed numerous "archeologies of knowledge" to show how moral, legal, and even scientific "discourses" developed as tools for the exercise of social power. Foucault's insights powered an emerging recognition of the ways in which notions of virtue, progress, liberty, science, and a whole litany of Western pieties have been used to justify European domination and exploitation of large parts of the globe. This is the animating insight behind the field of Postcolonial Studies, in the belly of which I found myself when I enrolled in the English PhD program at Columbia in 1995.

o o o

I almost didn't get into graduate school. Well, technically, I didn't get into graduate school.

As a college senior, I put most of my intellectual energy into a thesis on Jacques Derrida and the nature of textual signification in Plato and Saint Augustine. As the fall semester advanced, the idea of working up a résumé and looking for a job with my Comparative Literature degree was depressing. I could not

42. *On the Genealogy of Morals*, p. 107.
43. *On Truth and Untruth*, p. 47.

imagine turning my face away from the intellectual firehose to which it had been fixed for three and half years.

So I applied to graduate school. I was not motivated by a specific scholarly interest but by a fairly indiscriminate appetite for reading and thinking about big ideas. My application was a disaster. My personal statement could not describe my research interests. The fact was I that didn't have anything as definite as that. I was also too intimidated to ask the famous professors I was studying with for letters of recommendation. Instead, I asked professors with whom I felt a personal connection: one adjunct professor in Comparative Literature and two assistant professors who were headed, as it turned out, for denials of tenure.

So I didn't get in anywhere.

Then something happened. It went like this.

As a freshman, even before course registration had opened, I found a work-study job in the Dean of Students Office at the School of General Studies. One day, during my first semester, David Lelyveld, the Dean of Students, overheard me arguing some philosophical point with another work-study student who was an upperclassman. I don't remember the specifics of the argument, but I do remember that the long and winding debate took place by the file cabinets just outside Dean Lelyveld's office. I was doing my best to affect Socratic irony, assuming complete ignorance and asking innocent questions aimed at trapping my opponent in some fatal contradiction.

I can only imagine that I sounded both pompous and naïve. But David heard me with sympathy and took an interest in my intellectual development. He was always curious about what I thought of my courses and what I was reading. He would ask me probing questions and suggest interesting ways of thinking about what I was reading. I loved my interactions with him. He radiated integrity and kindness and seemed full of insight on every topic.

David is a historian of India and happened to be friends with Gayatri Spivak, of the English Department. Professor Spivak was one of the famous professors whom I thought of asking for a letter of recommendation. I had approached her about it one day before class but had gotten spooked when she said that while she was willing to write a recommendation for me, "the letter would be honest." I never followed up to ask for the letter, even when I got an "A" in the class.

When I told David that I hadn't gotten into the English PhD program at Columbia, he had said something vague about asking Gayatri if she had seen my application. One day, late in the spring, David told me that he had run into Gayatri on the train and that she'd said she'd talk to someone in the department that very day.

A few days later, I found a message on my answering machine from the tenured professor in the department who had supervised my senior thesis. He was calling to congratulate me on my "excellent senior essay" and to inform me that, after "a heartfelt appeal from Professor Spivak," the English Department was now prepared to offer me admission to the MA-PhD program. There was only one caveat: the MA year would not be funded; I'd have to pay for it myself. I was thrilled to accept the offer, took around $30,000 in student loans, and that was that.

I can't quite put into words the depth of gratitude I feel toward David and Gayatri.

o o o

Having entered graduate school on the wings of Deconstruction, I wrote a master's thesis on Plato's *Phaedrus*, offering a sort of friendly corrective to Derrida's famous reading in his 1972 book *Dissemination.*

My crush on Deconstruction and Postmodernism was real. The ripping open of conceptual categories, canons, and hierarchies has an intoxicating quality. So does the idea of putting one's scholarship in the service of dismantling systems of injustice and reducing human suffering. But eventually we had a falling out. I ran out of patience with the evasiveness, obfuscation, and intellectual vacuity of many of the leading voices in the field. I felt confident enough in my background in philosophy and theory to call bullshit where I saw it. And that's mainly what I saw.

o o o

The prevailing ethos in the academic humanities today takes for granted the dismantling of value-based judgments that I have associated with Nietzsche and Postmodernism. This is probably the main intellectual impediment to the kind of liberal arts education that I encountered in the Columbia Core Curriculum and which I have spent much of my professional life advocating.

The philosophical reduction of value judgment to questions of power undermines liberal education because the human good—the kind of life most worth living—is the central inquiry of liberal education. Liberal learning begins from the premise that a human life can be oriented toward virtue—that is, toward human excellence. It therefore makes the nature of the human good its central concern. To put it in Socrates's words, the whole project is about "which whole way of life would make living most worthwhile for each of us?"[44] But if all

---

44. Plato, *Republic*, G.M.A. Grube and C.D.C. Reeve, trans. (Indianapolis and Cambridge: Hackett Publishing Company, 1992), p. 21.

that can be discovered behind notions like virtue, truth, and the human good are hierarchies of social power, liberal education is at best an empty pursuit, at worst a bankrupt system for exploiting existing power structures.

Some might argue that a liberal education seeks precisely to bring students to see for themselves the contingency and instrumentality of all value systems—that liberal education is fundamentally critical and deconstructive, aimed at puncturing the pretensions of power elites and exposing the complicity of traditional hierarchies of value in systems of oppression and subjugation. This view evades the actual question of the human good by saying that, in effect, the question cannot be asked. Instead of inquiry into the character of a good life and how to live it, we are left with inquiry into the disguised operations of power and how to uncover them. On this view, a liberally educated person is one who is clear-eyed about the ultimate emptiness of any notion of the human good and who can see behind it the actual structures of power in the service of which it operates.

This "critical" view is problematic on several fronts, including the fact that it removes the possibility of making generalizable judgments about the ideas, texts, and debates that a liberal education curriculum should foreground. It is this view that makes Matthew Arnold's famous adage that liberal learning should consist in "getting to know the best which has been thought and said in the world" such an object of derision among academic humanists.[45] But Arnold was right about this, and every course offered

---

45. It's worth adding that Arnold was not proposing a mere veneration of the glories of the past. In fact, in his view, the whole point of getting to know "the best which has been thought and said in the world" was so that "through this knowledge," we may turn "a stream of fresh and free thought upon our stock notions and habits."

by any professor represents some instantiation of his dictum, even if the object of the course is to refute the dictum.

If we deny the capacity to make generalizable value judgments—albeit contestable and revisable ones—about what things from the past are most worth passing on to young people as they pursue "higher education," we lose the capacity to organize a liberal education curriculum. As indeed most institutions have.

A program in liberal education guided by the deconstructive approach to the question of value produces precisely the kind of incoherence and debility characteristic of general education programs across higher education. As a result, we find a mass exodus of students from the study of liberal arts and an endemic inability among liberal arts professors to offer compelling reasons for why they shouldn't leave.

Liberal education is not possible without a recognition that inquiry into the life of virtue—that is, into the best and most excellent life for a human being to live—is not a futile endeavor but, in fact, leads to a deeper self-understanding and, in this sense, a fuller life. By setting its sights on inquiry into the human good, liberal education takes seriously the possibility of such a thing and the viability of rational investigation into its character. Moreover, this inquiry into the human good cannot be merely an intellectual exercise; it must also be a way of life that is informed and shaped by the insights that this ongoing investigation yields.

Because it is ever-unfolding, liberal education cannot be conducted in the service of a predetermined notion of the human good. Liberal education lives in the questions, not in the answers. Except for the premise—which is itself contestable—that

---

Matthew Arnold, *Culture and Anarchy* (1869), Samuel Lipman, ed. (New Haven: Yale University Press, 1994), p. 5.

the best life for a human being must include conscious reflection on the nature of the human good, a liberal education does not specify the content of that good. Indeed, because of the variability and divergence of the various conceptions of the human good to which a liberal education exposes a student, liberal education, unless it devolves into indoctrination, becomes necessarily an education in the *contestability and incompleteness* of any account of the human good. Leo Strauss, who was famous for his veneration of classical texts, made this point in memorable terms:

> To repeat: liberal education consists in listening to the conversation among the greatest minds. But here we are confronted with the overwhelming difficulty that this conversation does not take place without our help—that in fact we must bring about that conversation. The greatest minds utter monologues. We must transform their monologues into dialogue, their "side by side" into "together" ... [And] since the greatest minds contradict one another regarding the most important matters, they compel us to judge of their monologues; we cannot take on trust what any one of them says.[46]

○ ○ ○

Gandhi would probably not even entertain the philosophical challenges to truth that continental European philosophy elaborated throughout the twentieth century. For him, the truth of truth was evident in the very fact of existence. As he often pointed out, the Sanskrit word for truth, *satya*, comes from the

---

46. Leo Strauss, "What Is Liberal Education?" in *Liberalism Ancient and Modern* (Chicago: University of Chicago Press, 1995), p. 7.

root *sat*, which means "to be" or "to exist."[47] For Gandhi, truth was the underlying condition of being. Humans, moreover, had the unique capacity to access and "realize" *satya* through devotion and self-purification.

Gandhi's interest in truth was decidedly non-theoretical. He was interested in the *practice* of truth. Even scouring the 100 volumes of his collected works, one would be hard-pressed to extract a metaphysical theory of truth to put next to philosophical approaches such as Plato's or Nietzsche's. Gandhi was, after all, primarily interested not in knowledge but in salvation. The ceaseless, practical, self-denying striving after truth, beginning with the simple fact of always telling the truth, would, in its fullness, blossom into the realization of *moksha*, the ultimate liberation from the cycle of death and rebirth.

The world Nietzsche describes as reducible to the will to power, Gandhi recognizes only as an aberration, as "the law of the jungle," which humanity largely superseded as it emerged from the darkness and unconsciousness of its animal past. All of human culture and civilization speaks to the triumph of *ahimsa*, with violence being the exception rather than the rule.

But one can also see a more fundamental agreement between the saint and the philosopher, for Gandhi sees truth and nonviolence also in terms of power—as "soul force." In his telling, soul force is actually the most powerful force in the universe. To this extent, Gandhi, too, is a theorist of power, though he conceives of power as an aspect of an even more fundamental reality: Truth.

∘ ∘ ∘

---

47. *Moral and Political Writings*, Vol. 2, p. 157.

In the first essay of *On the Genealogy of Morals*, Nietzsche tells the story of "the slave revolt in morality": "a revolt which has a history of two thousand years behind it and which we no longer see because—it has been victorious!"[48] This revolt overthrew a system of "master morality" that upheld prowess, strength, and conquest as its chief virtues. In its stead, the new morality— "slave morality"—enthroned selflessness, humility, and renunciation as its highest values.

Slave morality overcame master morality by deploying a more subtle but ultimately more effective form of power. Unable to physically conquer the masters, slaves turned their aggression inward, transforming their hostility into the powerful force Nietzsche called "resentment": "the profoundest and sublimest kind of hatred."[49] Driven by their impotent animosity, slaves executed "an act of the *most spiritual revenge*"—"a radical revaluation of their enemies' values."[50] Henceforth, what masters had considered "good" would be, in the slave morality that came to dominate European culture, "evil." The masters' prowess would now be aggression; their strength, violence.

Concepts from different philosophical worldviews never hold a one-to-one correspondence, but there is a clear kinship between that psychological power with which slaves transformed the values of the masters and Gandhi's notion of soul force. By investing their weakness and suffering with spiritual meaning and compelling the masters into an inner "revaluation" of their own values, Nietzsche's slaves exercised what Gandhi would clearly recognize as soul force.

---

48. *On the Genealogy of Morals*, p. 34.
49. *On the Genealogy of Morals*, p. 34.
50. *On the Genealogy of Morals*, p. 34; the emphasis is in the original.

In South Africa, Gandhi gave the power based on adherence to truth and non-violence its own name: satyagraha. "Satyagraha is soul force pure and simple," he wrote in his history of the South African movement.[51] He chose the term because of the inadequacy of the closest English equivalent—"passive resistance"—which "was supposed to be a weapon of the weak":[52]

> As the struggle advanced, the phrase [passive resistance] gave rise to confusion, and it appeared shameful to permit this great struggle to be known only by an English name. . . . A small prize was therefore announced in *Indian Opinion* to be awarded to the reader who invented the best designation for the struggle. . . . Shri Maganlal Gandhi was one of the competitors and he suggested the word *sadagraha*, meaning "firmness in a good cause." I liked the word but it did not fully represent the whole idea I wished to connote. I therefore corrected it to "satyagraha." Truth (*satya*) implies love, and firmness (*agraha*) engenders and therefore serves as a synonym for force. I thus began to call the Indian movement "satyagraha," that is to say, the Force which is born of Truth and Love or Non-violence.[53]

Gandhi's conception of soul force embodies one of the many counterintuitive principles by which he operated: that the only legitimate power one can exercise over another is one's willingness to suffer and thereby appeal to, and transform, the other's inner disposition. "Satyagraha postulates the conquest of the adversary by suffering in one's own person," he wrote, emphasizing

---

51. Mohandas K. Gandhi, *Satyagraha in South Africa*, CWMG, Vol. 29, p. 95.
52. *Autobiography*, p. 284.
53. *Satyagraha in South Africa*, CWMG, Vol. 29, p. 92.

the difference between satyagraha and physical force.[54] Gandhi argued—some would say that he demonstrated—that the acceptance of suffering in upholding a just cause unleashes an irresistible power, the very moral force that, as *satya*, sustains the universe. "Real suffering bravely born melts even a heart of stone. Such is the potency of suffering or *tapas*. And there lies the key to Satyagraha."[55]

Satyagraha can be offered by individuals in strictly personal matters, such as in domestic disputes, as well as on a mass scale, such as Gandhi organized against South African authorities and, eventually, against British rule in India. In both cases, Gandhi's basic approach was to steel masses of people to accept punishment for violations of laws that they believed were unjust. "If I do not obey a law, and accept the penalty for its breach, I use soul force. It involves sacrifice of self."[56] The Gandhian calculus is that, when faced with the naked demonstration of the injustice of a law in the form of innocent suffering in resistance to it, no human authority can long keep its nerve, and no bystander can long remain neutral. Non-violent non-cooperation—satyagraha—directs the moral force of the universe against injustice. Because "violence dies when it ceases to evoke response from its object,"[57] Gandhi's unshakable faith was that non-violent satyagraha would always win, even in the face of repression.

o o o

54. *Satyagraha in South Africa*, CWMG, Vol. 29, p. 96.

55. *Satyagraha in South Africa*, CWMG, Vol. 29, p. 18.

56. *Hind Swaraj and Other Writings*, p. 90.

57. Mohandas K. Gandhi, "To Young Bengal," *Young India* (Jan. 19, 1921); CWMG, Vol. 19, p. 233.

Gandhi worked out the basic tenets of his personal and political religion in South Africa. In the twenty-one years he spent there, he underwent a personal transformation of the deepest order, including adoption of his four rules of conduct: truthfulness, non-violence, celibacy, and non-possession. He also changed his appearance: "During the Satyagraha in South Africa, I had altered my style of dress so as to make it more in keeping with that of the indentured laborers."[58] For the rest of his life, Gandhi's dress became a recognizable symbol of his identification with the poor and destitute. The man who returned to India for good in 1915 was the fully formed spiritual radical and mass organizer upon whom the poet Rabindranath Tagore would confer the honorific title of Mahatma a few years later.

As a London-educated barrister in South Africa, Gandhi found himself in a position to represent a community of indentured servants and poor Indian workers who were otherwise politically voiceless. From his earliest experiences in this role, he understood his function as one that hinged on organizing masses of people around simple objectives whose moral foundations were clear. This allowed him to cast his political activism on behalf of the dispossessed as a religious mission. "The struggle for human liberty," he often repeated, "is a religious struggle."[59]

Gandhi spent his first year back in India under a vow taken before his political mentor Gopal Krishna Gokhale, a leading figure in the Indian National Congress, not to make any political pronouncements or join any movement. Instead, he undertook a grand listening tour, traveling the length of the country as a third-class passenger and suffering the indignities of the poorest of the poor in a brutally hierarchical society. His goal, as it had been in

---

58. *Autobiography*, p. 337.
59. *CWMG*, Vol. 12, p. 276.

South Africa, was to identify with the masses so thoroughly as to absorb their hardships into his personal struggle for religious liberation. His own *swaraj* would thereby involve the emancipation of India's "half-starved, half-naked dumb millions."

Swaraj ("self-governance") became the banner term under which Gandhi pursued his political "experiments." In India, he also began to use the word to describe his ultimate spiritual goal: "Government over self is the truest *swaraj*. It is synonymous with *moksha* or salvation," he wrote in *Young India* in late 1920.[60] *Swaraj* came to encompass political independence from British rule as well as personal liberation from spiritual bondage. Indeed, Gandhi insisted on the inextricability of these two conditions. "If we become free," he wrote in *Hind Swaraj*, "India is free . . . in this thought you have the definition of Swaraj. It is Swaraj when we learn to rule ourselves. It is, therefore, in the palm of our hands."[61]

Independence from England, in Gandhi's vision, was not the ultimate goal of his "constructive program," but a byproduct of the religious revival he sought to spark—an awakening that would transcend and heal the deepest divisions in Indian society: those between Hindus and Muslims, those between caste Hindus and untouchables, and those between India's elite and its destitute masses. Solving these essentially internal Indian problems, Gandhi insisted, must precede *swaraj*, and, in fact, those solutions were the conditions for the *swaraj* he sought. "If we desist from our sins, the Government will drop off like dead leaves," he argued.[62]

---

60. Mohandas K. Gandhi, *Young India* (Dec. 8, 1920); *CWMG*, Vol. 19, p. 80.

61. *Hind Swaraj and Other Writings*, p. 73.

62. Mohandas K. Gandhi, "Non Co-operation means Self-Purification," *Navajivan* (Jan. 27, 1921); *CWMG*, Vol. 19, p. 284.

This vision helps explain why Gandhi's program to achieve Indian home rule at first sight seems to have little to do with Britain. His program for "parliamentary *swaraj*"—which became a national program when he assumed leadership of the Indian National Congress in 1920—rested on "four pillars": spinning for at least half an hour every day and wearing exclusively homespun cloth; abolishing untouchability from Hinduism; establishing unity among the various religious communities, especially between Hindus and Muslims; and renouncing all violence as a means of achieving political ends. One might wonder what any of those reforms had to do with independence from British rule. Everything, Gandhi would say: "If India adopted the doctrine of love as an active part of her religion and introduced it in her politics, Swaraj would descend upon India from heaven."[63]

Swaraj, for Gandhi, meant liberation from the materialist and acquisitive drive that he saw at the heart of European civilization. In his view, it was by surrendering to these spiritual vices that India became subservient in the first place: "The English have not taken India; we have given it to them," he wrote in *Hind Swaraj*,[64] adding that "the English entered India for the purposes of trade. They remain in it for the same purpose, and we help them to do so. Their arms and ammunition are perfectly useless."[65] This searing insight drives Gandhi's conviction that the path to non-violent *swaraj* consists in weaning India from its addiction to Western materialism: "It is my deliberate opinion that India is being

63. Mohandas K. Gandhi, "Hind Swaraj" or the "Indian Home Rule," *Young India* (Jan. 26, 1921); *CWMG*, Vol. 19, p. 278.

64. *Hind Swaraj and Other Writings*, p. 39.

65. *Hind Swaraj and Other Writings*, p. 41.

ground down not under the English heel but under that of modern civilization."[66]

o o o

Gandhi had a lot to say about modern civilization (or Western or European civilization—he used these terms interchangeably). His first and essential book, *Hind Swaraj*, written in 1909 as he returned to South Africa from a trip to England, is primarily an invective against Western civilization. It is, in large part, a condemnation of modernity itself.

Gandhi's rejection of modern civilization would be recognizable to us as a critique of capitalism. He judged modern civilization primarily by its economic system—which is to say, in terms of the ascendance of materialism and a commodity-based value system that he saw pervading the whole culture.

In rejecting Western civilization, Gandhi does not have in mind the classical tradition—he was a great admirer of Socrates and other ancient writers. Nor does he repudiate its religious traditions—he admired all of the Abrahamic faiths. Moreover, he embraced that strand of modern anti-materialist Western thought that includes Leo Tolstoy, John Ruskin, and Henry David Thoreau—all of whom Gandhi counted as among his most important influences. What Gandhi, in fact, rejected in Western civilization is the mode of life and social organization that emerged from the Industrial Revolution: "Let it be remembered," he wrote in his South African journal *Indian Opinion* in 1908, "that western civilization is only a hundred years old, or to be more precise, fifty."[67]

---

66. *Hind Swaraj and Other Writings*, p. 42.
67. *CWMG*, Vol. 8, p. 374.

In other words, what Gandhi means by Western civilization is not Jerusalem, Athens, or Rome, but a modern way of life that places comfort, security, and longevity as its chief goods. In *Hind Swaraj*, he argued that what today is considered "civilization" refers simply to "the fact that people living in it make bodily welfare the object of life."[68] The roots of this materialist orientation in European culture lie in the rationalist philosophy of Enlightenment thinkers like René Descartes and Francis Bacon. It is the same philosophical matrix that spawned the research ideal dominant in today's university.

Gandhi sees the gains of modern civilization as hollow and as depending on the exploitation of the common laborer:

> A man labouring under the bane of civilization is like a dreaming man. . . . Now, thousands of workmen meet together and for the sake of maintenance work in factories or mines. Their condition is worse than that of beasts. . . . Formerly men were made slaves under physical compulsion, now they are enslaved by temptation of money and of the luxuries that money can buy. . . . Civilization seeks to increase bodily comforts, and it fails miserably even in doing so.[69]

The brutalization of the common worker under the free market system is something that the great theorizer of capitalism Adam Smith saw clearly himself:

> In the progress of the division of labour, the employment of the far greater part of those who live by labour, that is, of the great body of the people, comes to be confined to a few very simple operations, frequently to one or two. . . . The

---

68. *Hind Swaraj and Other Writings*, p. 35.
69. *Hind Swaraj and Other Writings*, p. 35.

man whose whole life is spent in performing a few simple operations . . . generally becomes as stupid and ignorant as it is possible for a human creature to become. The torpor of his mind renders him not only incapable of relishing or bearing a part in any rational conversation, but of conceiving any generous, noble, or tender sentiment, and consequently of forming any just judgment concerning many even of the ordinary duties of private life. . . . His dexterity at his own particular trade seems, in this manner, to be acquired at the expense of his intellectual, social, and martial virtues. But in every improved and civilised society this is the state into which the labouring poor, that is, the great body of the people, must necessarily fall, unless government takes some pains to prevent it.[70]

It is his repudiation of this economic system—whose implications for the common worker Smith saw so presciently—that ultimately brought Gandhi to an all-out campaign to end British rule in India. Already in 1921, not long after assuming leadership of the Indian National Congress, he wrote in *Young India*: "Our non-cooperation is neither with the English nor with the West. Our non-cooperation is with the system the English have established, with the material civilization and its attendant greed and exploitation of the weak."[71]

o o o

The "material civilization" Gandhi condemns is the product, like the research university, of the epistemological shifts we

70. Adam Smith, *The Wealth of Nations*, Book 5 (New York: Random House, Modern Library, 2000), p. 840.

71. Mohandas K. Gandhi, *Young India* (Oct. 13, 1921); CWMG, Vol. 21, p. 291.

associate with the Scientific Revolution of the sixteenth and seventeenth centuries. While unlocking our capacity to manipulate nature and extract goods from the environment in spectacular ways, the scientific paradigm that came to dominate Western learning also holds a poison pill. It offers an answer to the fundamental question of liberal education—what kind of life is most worth living?—in purely materialistic terms: the life most worth living is a long life that enjoys all of the comforts and pleasures that our ability to manipulate the environment can bring us.

René Descartes is perhaps the most influential architect of the philosophical underpinnings of this view. In his foundational *Discourse on the Method for Conducting One's Reason Well and for Seeking Truth in the Sciences* (1637), he urges against the fruitless speculations and debates of the humanistic philosophical tradition he inherited and calls for a re-orientation of learning toward the amelioration of the ills that beset human life:

> Knowing the force and the actions of fire, water, air, the stars, the heavens, and all the other bodies that surround us . . . [we] render ourselves, as it were, masters and possessors of nature. This is desirable not only for the invention of an infinity of devices that would enable one to enjoy trouble-free the fruits of the earth and all the goods found there, but also principally for the maintenance of health, which unquestionably is the first good and the foundation of all the other goods of this life. . . . . one could rid oneself of an infinity of maladies, as much of the body as of the mind, and even perhaps also the frailty of old age, if one had a sufficient knowledge of their causes and of all the remedies that nature has provided us.

Having glimpsed the Faustian possibility of solving, scientifically, the riddle of aging, sickness, and perhaps even death, Descartes forms the "intention of spending my entire life in the search for so indispensable a science," and he calls upon all "good minds to try to advance beyond this [his own discoveries] by contributing, each according to his inclination and ability, to the experiments that must be performed."[72]

Today, the heirs to Descartes's project are perhaps most visible in Silicon Valley, but the ethic that informs his approach is pervasive in the broader culture, including the culture of the university. This view places a long and comfortable life as the ultimate goal of the search for knowledge, recognizing no higher value than the subsistence and satisfaction of the self. Gandhi saw this conception of the ends of a human life as inevitably leading to the exploitation of the natural environment, of fellow living creatures, and, ultimately, of fellow human beings. Writing publicly to the Gujarati scholar Narasinhrao Divetiya, Gandhi spells out his understanding of this dominant cultural paradigm:

> By Western civilization I mean the ideals which people in the West have embraced in modern times and the pursuits based on these ideals. The supremacy of brute force, worshipping money as God, spending most of one's time in seeking worldly happiness, breath-taking risks in pursuit of worldly enjoyments of all kinds, the expenditure of limitless mental energy on efforts to multiply the power of machinery, the expenditure of crores on the invention of means of destruction, the moral righteousness which looks down upon people outside Europe,—this civilization, in my view, deserves to be altogether rejected.[73]

---

72. René Descartes, *Discourse on Method and Meditations on First Philosophy*, 4th ed., Donald A. Cress, trans. (Indianapolis and Cambridge: Hackett Publishing Company, 1998), p. 35.

73. Mohandas K. Gandhi, "To the Learned Narasinhrao," *Navajivan* (Dec. 29, 1920); *CWMG*, Vol. 19, p. 178.

The unrestrained pursuit of physical comforts, pleasures, material goods, and long life, are, for Gandhi, inextricably linked to violence. A civilization built around these goals will inevitably depend on brute force to defend and advance its aims, with no higher authority than its own interests to constrain its actions. With his own eyes, Gandhi saw that modern civilization was sustained by egregious amounts of violence against the natural world and against fellow human beings. In his conviction that the exploitation of others is inexorably baked into the economic structure of Western civilization, Gandhi can sound positively Marxist.

Against the Western materialist account of the highest human good, Gandhi proposed a view that breaks with the dominant humanism and individualism of the West. His conception of the good extended not only beyond the individual, but beyond the human species. In the *Autobiography*, he noted that "to my mind the life of a lamb is no less precious than that of a human being. I should be unwilling to take the life of a lamb for the sake of the human body."[74] This sentiment—pervasive in Gandhi's writings and in how he organized his life—highlights just how profoundly he diverges from the dominant premises of the tradition traced in courses like Introduction to Contemporary Civilization in the West, in which the unique value of human life is almost universally assumed. It also illustrates why Gandhi's addition to the required readings in the Columbia course is so enriching.

Gandhi's non-humanist conception of the human good is again evident in his rejection of violence even in self-defense. In a striking passage responding to a correspondent's question pressing him on this point, Gandhi lays out his views:

---

74. *Autobiography*, p. 208.

I do not want to live at the cost of even the life of a snake. I should let him bite me to death rather than kill him. But it is likely that if God puts me to that cruel test and permits a snake to assault me, I may not have to courage to die but the beast within me may assert itself and I may seek to kill the snake in defending this perishable body. I admit that my belief has not become so incarnate as to warrant my stating emphatically that I have shed all fear of snakes so as to befriend them as I would like to be able to do.[75]

For Gandhi, taking a life, even in self-defense, is always a moral failure, as the search for truth necessarily involves the assiduous practice of non-violence (*ahimsa*). Violence, for him, is always an attack on truth; violence is always *violence against truth*: "*Ahimsa* and Truth are so intertwined that it is practically impossible to disentangle and separate them."[76]

In Gandhi's view, life's highest good is not life as such, but a virtuous life, and human virtue involves the acceptance of limits on what one is willing to do to stay alive. In this, Gandhi coincides with Socrates, who rejects the chance to escape death by reminding Crito that "the most important thing is not life, but the good life."[77] For Gandhi, a good life includes the "demand at some stage—an inexorable demand—that we should cease to kill our fellow creatures for satisfaction of bodily wants."[78]

o o o

75. *CWMG*, Vol. 33, p. 234.

76. Letter to Narandas Gandhi (July 28, 1931); *CWMG*, Vol. 44, p. 59.

77. *Crito*, 48b, p. 48, in Plato, *The Trial and Death of Socrates*, trans. by G.M.A Grube, rev. by John M. Cooper, 3rd ed. (Indianapolis and Cambridge: Hackett Publishing Company, 2000).

78. *Moral and Political Writings*, Vol. 2, p. 169.

In one of the many moments in the *Autobiography* when Gandhi steps aside from the narrative in order to reflect on matters of broader importance, he asks, "How heavy is the toll of sins and wrongs that wealth, power and prestige exact from man?"[79] I cannot read Gandhi—nor can many of my students—without asking that question not of humanity in general but of the particular human that I am. Is there a toll of sin and wrong associated with whatever wealth, power, or prestige I enjoy? While the terms "sins" and "wrongs" do not carry the same force for me that they did for Gandhi, I cannot escape the cascade of issues that his question provokes: To what extent do my material advantages, my professional accomplishments, my social privileges, depend on the exploitation, marginalization, and exclusion of others? To what extent do I sacrifice truth, integrity, or self-respect in pursuit of personal and career advancement? How far and how frequently do I accept degrading compromises to my sense of right? To what degree do I live a compromised life? And what is the cost of such a life?

I don't raise these questions in order to acquit myself. They are some of the most uncomfortable questions that I live with. They are questions that Gandhi forces me to ask. They are questions that I hope my students also feel inspired to ask of themselves after reading Gandhi. They are among the questions that a liberal education in the midst of modern civilization must raise for each individual. Like Socrates, who, in the *Apology*, chided Athenians for their "eagerness to possess as much wealth, reputation and honors as possible" while giving little "thought to wisdom or truth, or the best possible state of your soul,"[80] Gandhi

---

79. *Autobiography*, p. 203.

80. *Apology*, 29d–30b, p. 32, in Plato, *The Trial and Death of Socrates*, trans. by G.M.A Grube, rev. by John M. Cooper, 3rd ed. (Indianapolis and Cambridge: Hackett Publishing Company, 2000).

confronts a contemporary reader with an age-old liberal arts question: To what extent does advancing my material interests compromise my spiritual well-being?

The frequent zero-sum economy between material and spiritual interest is not accidental; the two modes of pursuit seem indissolubly linked and frequently incompatible. As Jesus said, "No one can serve two masters; for either he will hate the one and love the other, or he will be devoted to one and despise the other. You cannot serve God and wealth."[81] Or, as articulated by the eighth-century Chinese poet Du Fu:

After the laws of their being,
All creatures pursue happiness.
Why have I let an official
Career swerve me from my goal?[82]

o o o

Personally, Gandhi reawakened a deep sense of spirituality for me. Around the time I started reading him, I took up the practice of mediation and a meandering, unmethodical, but sustained exploration of Buddhism. Like Gandhi, I have to say that "I do not believe in a personal deity." But his commitment to "the Eternal Law of Truth and Love translated as non-violence"[83] touches a reality I sense in the deepest part of my being.

---

81. Matthew 6:24 (New American Standard Bible).

82. Du Fu, "By the Winding River II," in *One Hundred Poems from the Chinese*, Kenneth Rexroth, trans. (New York: New Directions, 1971), p. 14.

83. *Moral and Political Writings*, Vol. 2, p. 192.

EPILOGUE

Nuts and Bolts

As an undergraduate at Columbia thirty years ago, the Core Curriculum helped me make sense of the adult world into which I was entering. Even for students for whom college does not involve as drastic a cultural adaptation as it did for me, programs like the Columbia Core provide the intellectual framework for a lifetime of growth and development. But the Core Curriculum also draws a lot of criticism. Sometimes I compare it to a lightning rod, which attracts high-voltage discharges from the clouds and, in doing so, protects the house in which we live.

My years as Director of the Center for the Core Curriculum were immersed in the intellectual debates and institutional complexities surrounding the Core. Given Columbia's emphasis on the "Western tradition," for example, I often had to contend with accusations that liberal education was, in fact, indoctrination in Western values. I encountered this criticism from predictable sources, like Chinese government bureaucrats wary of the introduction of American-style liberal education in Chinese universities. I also encountered it from people championing voices and interests that have been historically marginalized in the "Western tradition"—women and people of color especially.

In responding to these criticisms, I had to make two arguments at once. One is that a liberal education does not need to be, as it is at Columbia, centered on "Western" classics. The second is that "Western" texts and debates, in fact, underpin much of the emerging global culture and that their importance, especially in Western societies, is inescapable. Contemporary notions like human rights, democracy, gender equality, scientific objectivity, the free market, equality before the law, and many others, cannot be adequately accounted for without studying the "Western tradition." To be sure, "the West" does not contain the only important contributions to these notions, but it does contain decisive ones.

"The West" as a category is, of course, itself problematic. For one thing, no large cultural formation has ever developed in isolation, and none can be treated as a separate and self-contained unit. For another, the banners of "Western civilization" and "Western culture" have been used to give cover to imperialist, racist, and colonialist agendas and to justify the subjugation and exploitation of "non-Western" people. In many cases, "Western civilization" has simply been the name given to an ideology of white racial supremacy and European domination. So one has to hold the phrase, as it were, at arm's length.

But the term is also used to describe something more legitimate: a large and porous cultural configuration around the Mediterranean Sea, with strong Greco-Roman roots, that served as the historical seedbed for the Renaissance, the Enlightenment, the Scientific Revolution, the Industrial Revolution, and much of what is called "modernity."[1] While the European continent figures prominently, the tradition incorporates

---

1. Like "Western," many of these terms are themselves only shorthand for complex and sometimes loose configurations of related historical phenomena.

defining elements from non-European sources like the Arab world, ancient Egypt and north Africa, and even the far East.

Used in this way, the term simply describes an integrated tradition of learning, debate, artistic expression, and political evolution. But while it is an integrated tradition, it is by no means a monolithic tradition—in fact, one of its hallmarks is its internal contentiousness. It is a tradition rife with fissures, where overturning the past is preferred to venerating it. Key aspects of the modern world emerge from this tradition of contest and debate, loose and fractured as it is. The case for its importance in understanding our emerging global culture is overwhelming. The tradition matters not because it is Western, but because of its contribution to human questions of the highest order.

One of the strongest currents in this tradition is *textual*—a documentary lineage of literary, philosophical, and artistic reflections stretching as far back as Homer and the pre-Socratic philosophers. This documentary tradition is a long and contentious conversation about fundamental aspects of human life. It is, roughly, what the Columbia Core Curriculum organizes into a program of general education. Its four required humanities courses (two of them year-long), present students, in chronological order, with major texts in literature (Literature Humanities), ethics and politics (Contemporary Civilization), visual art (Art Humanities), and music (Music Humanities). The full names of these courses, the youngest of which goes back seventy-five years, recall a time of relative consensus on matters now highly disputed: Masterpieces of European Literature and Philosophy, Introduction to Contemporary Civilization in the West, Masterpieces of Western Art, and Masterpieces of Western Music.[2]

---

2. Here's a curious story. In a Nov. 26, 2016, column ("Election Therapy from My Basket of Deplorables"), *New York Times* columnist Maureen Dowd presented her

The focus of the Columbia Core Curriculum on the "Western tradition" is perhaps its most criticized feature. My own view is that while there is no justification for an *exclusively* Western liberal arts curriculum, there is a compelling case for keeping the Western tradition at the center of general education, at least in the West. In other words, in today's world, the Western tradition is essential, but not sufficient.

Columbia has long been aware of this deficiency and has made repeated attempts to incorporate non-Western perspectives in the undergraduate curriculum, including the heroic and decades-long efforts of William Theodore DeBary to create courses in non-Western classics that parallel the required Core and give students access to other major traditions of learning.[3] Columbia's current and, to my mind, insufficient corrective to its Western-heavy Core Curriculum is a distribution requirement whereby students must complete two semesters of coursework that deal with, loosely speaking, non-Western primary sources. Since 2008, this requirement has been called the Global Core.

---

conservative brother's "annual holiday column." In it, Kevin Dowd chided the liberal establishment for its disconnection from and condescension toward mainstream America. Among his condemnations of liberal culture was the claim that "not one of the top 50 colleges mandate one semester of Western Civilization." In response to my letter to the editor challenging this claim, Ms. Dowd and her fact-checker defended the statement, pointing to a 2011 report by the National Association of Scholars (NAS), a conservative advocacy group. NAS would not consider Columbia's Introduction to Contemporary Civilization in the West as a course in "Western Civilization" because its required reading list included the *Holy Qur'an*.

3. When I began my tenure as Director of the Center for the Core Curriculum in 2008, it was my earnest ambition to expand the Core to include versions of these non-Western courses as common requirements for undergraduates. My inability to make significant progress in this direction was an education in university administration. But that would have to be the subject of a separate essay.

o o o

Columbia's required Core Curriculum, weighted toward the past and therefore toward "dead white males," also invites questions about inclusivity, diversity, and representation. Students never fail to ask these questions, *and they are right to ask them.* The very existence of a core curriculum puts the question of what is most worthwhile for all students to study front and center, forcing the faculty and administrators to address it directly among themselves and in an ongoing dialogue with students and the public. A core curriculum requires that an institution think concretely about the meaning of general education and clarify for itself the values that inform its curricular choices. It also requires faculty to think beyond their discipline and articulate their own specialized concerns within a broad framework of what a generally educated person ought to know.

At Columbia, debates about exclusion, hegemony, and representation are an inherent aspect of the Core Curriculum. They are integral to, rather than a distraction from, the liberal education that the Core delivers. They are, as programmers say, a feature, not a bug. The Core is not a thing that is set and done, but an ongoing reflective endeavor that demands constant reassessment, adjustment, and justification. Those of us who believe in the value of a liberal education based in the study of important texts from the past—a core curriculum—must be prepared to explain our curricular choices, defend them, and, when they don't stand up to scrutiny, revise them.

The often uncomfortable and sometimes perilous task of defending a particular common curriculum points to one of the reasons they are so rare. At most institutions, faculty and administrators have decided that arguments and defenses for a specific required curriculum are not worth the trouble, and have simply replaced required courses with distribution requirements—and sometimes no requirements at all—that allow students—and allow faculty—to stay within their chosen intellectual comfort zones. It's an understandable decision, but one that shirks a basic responsibility of the faculty and which, in the long run, does a disservice to the students, to the institution, and to society. The problems of representation raised by a curriculum weighted toward the past must be solved by means other than the abandonment of the textual tradition that underpins contemporary life.

In over a decade of conversations with students about the required Core Curriculum at Columbia, I have typically found them to be honest, serious, and animated by a deep sense of justice. While they can be self-righteous and off target in their diagnoses and demands, I have also found them to be hungry for, and appreciative of, honest and non-condescending debate.

My approach has always been to welcome students aboard the task of thinking about the nature, goals, and rationale for a required set of courses. There's a large body of scholarship about these issues, and as with the rest of the Core, engagement with it allows student to develop informed opinions and to contribute fresh insights to the debate. As director of the program, I saw these conversations with students as an extension of the work I did in the classroom, and found them to be no less enriching and, on occasion, just as transformative as classroom teaching.

In my years in the "hot seat," as it were, I found students, as a rule, to be highly receptive to the logic that organizes the Core once it is presented lucidly, honestly, and non-defensively. The fact that I am myself a person of color was always helpful in these conversations in that it helped some students be more open to what I had to say and more willing to engage in good-faith dialogue.

Versions of these conversations happen wherever Core programs exist. Fostering a community-wide discussion that demands clarity and conviction is part of the educational function of a common curriculum. Every year, I held ongoing discussions with student groups and met individually with dozens of students. In times of particular tension, I brought together faculty and students to talk, listen, and think together about the issues at stake in offering a common core curriculum. We didn't always reach a happy agreement, but I don't believe anyone ever walked away from our conversations feeling disrespected, ignored, or maliciously sidelined.

At Columbia, I would often begin these conversations by explaining my role as director. I was the head *administrator* of the program; I did not determine its content nor dictate its shape. No one, in fact, does. The Core, especially its content, represents a loose and shifting consensus among the instructors who teach it. It was important for students to understand that the Core evolved over decades of debate and experimentation and that it has never obeyed the vision of any single individual or interest group. I would then explain the logic of the Core's curricular organization. What follows is an overview of that logic. I offer it as a model that has proven durable and extraordinarily successful.

The four humanities courses in the Core curriculum offer an overview of important works in the Western tradition from antiquity to the present. They are taught in seminars of around twenty students each, so that the entire student body of Columbia College has the experience of examining roughly the same works at the same time in small, discussion-driven classes. Because of their chronological organization, the courses reflect a history of intellectual and artistic production that, until at least the nineteenth century, largely excluded women, poor people, people of color, and non-elites in general, except as represented by the dominant voices. When the courses reach the nineteenth and twentieth centuries, the range of voices expands dramatically, reflecting new cultural configurations, so that contemporary questions like race, gender, and colonialism take center stage by the end of the year-long courses.

While the content of the Columbia Core Curriculum—the books and works students discuss—undergoes constant revision, the program maintains a set of commitments that have guided its evolution for over 100 years. I group these commitments into three categories: form, content, and revision.

Form

When it comes to form, the Core maintains:

1. *Small classes.* The current maximum number of students in a Core class is twenty-two. Small classes are absolutely necessary to develop the kind of intimacy between instructor and student and among students themselves that is the vehicle through which a liberal education occurs. It is also a precondition for the second aspect of the Core's commitments to form:
2. *Discussion* (rather than lectures). The Core instructor does not present him or herself as an expert but as a facilitator of conversation about issues raised by the text under discussion. It is the active and engaged participation of each member of the group that constitutes a Core class. Knowledge is not transmitted from teacher to student but constructed by the group through a shared process of inquiry and reflection.

A great part of the skill of a Core instructor concerns the ability to draw students into honest and open discussion of fundamental issues and to maintain an atmosphere in which a full range of opinions can be expressed and examined.

3. *Non-disciplinarity*. Core instructors come from all academic disciplines, and while each brings specific disciplinary perspectives, the courses themselves are pre-disciplinary—that is, they occupy the ground from which the disciplines arise. Their goal is to introduce students not to the academic disciplines, but to the intellectual problems that motivate them. This commitment to non-disciplinarity has an enriching effect on the faculty who teach in the Core. One of the most remarkable scenes in American higher education occurs every week in the Core conference room in Hamilton Hall, when faculty from different departments, different disciplinary training, and different stages of the academic career gather over lunch to discuss how to teach a Core text to undergraduates who are reading it for the first time.

4. *Commonality*. A frequent quip among Columbia instructors who teach advanced undergraduates is that we know exactly what each student has forgotten. The shared intellectual background of the Core opens unique pedagogical possibilities. When I teach the American Revolution in my senior seminar, I know that students have read Locke, as well as Hobbes, Rousseau, Smith, and Marx. When I discuss American slavery, I know that students have grappled with Aristotle's claims about natural slavery and with W.E.B. Du Bois's reflections on the black experience in America.

Beyond its intellectual benefits, the common intellectual experience is also a powerful creator of community, equipping students who may come from different backgrounds with a common vocabulary with which to talk across differences. Similarly, the Core provides a link among alumni and between alumni and the institution. As Columbia development officers readily admit, the Core is their most powerful tool for cultivating alumni relations.

Content

As for content, the Core is committed to:

1. *Core texts*, that is, works of major cultural significance—a designation that is, of course, always open to debate and revision.
2. *A chronological presentation*. Each course begins in antiquity and moves toward the present, drawing connections among texts and paying attention to the evolution of ideas and debates. This approach, as noted, means that elite white men dominate the syllabus, reflecting the social conditions of intellectual production for much of Western history. But this deficiency is an occasion to examine both the mechanisms by which that status quo has been maintained and the ways in which it has always been challenged. As in other cases, this task requires a high level of skill and sensitivity from the instructor.
3. *Western focus*. In important ways, the Core is a genealogy of the present. As such, it focuses on the lineage of thought and debate that has most directly shaped the Western world. If the Columbia Core were being created from scratch today, it would probably attempt to incorporate other world traditions. As noted, Columbia has supplemented the Western focus of the Core with a distribution requirement called the Global Core in which students study non-Western primary sources in a discussion-based format.

Revision

Lastly, the Core is committed to ongoing revision. In the case of the two-year-long humanities courses, the list of works read by all students is revised every three years, with a faculty-wide vote determining the set of works to be included in any given cycle. A syllabus revision is typically spearheaded by a small committee of faculty representing a broad range of disciplines and expertise. This committee will invite all faculty who teach in the course to propose changes to the syllabus, often reminding them of the importance of the teaching criterion: we want not just books that deserve the attention of undergraduates, but books that work well in the classroom—books that are "teachable." On the basis of the feedback gathered and of its members' own experience teaching in the Core, the committee will produce a draft new syllabus. This draft syllabus is then subjected to scrutiny by the entire faculty teaching in the Core in various town-hall-style meetings. From this process, a final proposed new syllabus emerges. The faculty then votes on whether to adopt this new syllabus or keep the old. In every vote that I know of, the consultative process that produced the new syllabus also ensured a strong vote in its favor. Hence change and reconsideration of the works included in the Core is ongoing and reflects continuous reassessments of what matters most about the past.

Starting from these commitments, my discussions with students and faculty about the shape and evolution of the Core have always been productive. These commitments are themselves up for debate, but they hold up well as flexible general principles. They are not cosmetic but require a significant investment of material and human resources by the institution. Students and alumni recognize this. In the periodic budget crises that invariably hit the University, students and alumni emerge as the fiercest defenders of these commitments. While not every institution can implement a Columbia-style Core Curriculum, the commitments that underlie it can be adapted almost everywhere to deliver the kind of liberal education I have advocated in this book.

o o o

Columbia's Core Curriculum is the oldest and perhaps the most influential general education program in higher education. It has served, and continues to serve, as a model for many liberal arts programs in the United States and abroad.[4] Many of its faculty and student alumni have become ambassadors for a Core-text approach to liberal education.

I have myself traveled extensively in the US and abroad to talk to faculty, students, and administrations about liberal education based on the study of important texts. Almost everywhere I go, people are curious about, and then surprised by, what Columbia does for a core curriculum. I also often hear, almost reflexively, that the Columbia model is impractical and could not be implemented anywhere else. This easy dismissal comes in various flavors—that such programs are too expensive, that no professors would want to teach them, that students won't want to take them, that college students in any but the

---

4. In recent decades, there has been a marked interest, from universities abroad, in the American liberal arts model. I have been fortunate to help launch three notable programs inspired by the Columbia Core Curriculum: the General Education Program at the Chinese University of Hong Kong (https://www.cuhk.edu.hk/334/english/university-core/general-education.html), the Core Curriculum at Shalem College in Jerusalem (https://shalem.ac.il/en/core-program/), and the Core Curriculum at Universidad Adolfo Ibañez in Santiago, Chile (https://artesliberales.uai.cl/core-curriculum/).

most elite colleges lack the intellectual preparation to benefit from such programs.

I readily grant that the Columbia program cannot be easily replicated. And if it were, I would not advocate for its wholesale replication. There is no one-size-fits-all formula for a program in general education. Every institution's approach must emerge organically from its faculty, its resources, its traditions, and its values. But the broad set of principles and practices that guide the Columbia model can, and should be, widely adopted. Among these principles and practices are the focus on texts of major cultural significance, small classes conducted as conversations rather than lectures, commonality of intellectual experience among students, and non-disciplinarity in choice of materials and methods of engagement.

Columbia, though iconic for the longevity and extent of its Core Curriculum, is far from alone in offering a general education that embodies these principles of liberal arts pedagogy. Many schools and many different kinds of schools do so to various degrees. Some of these programs are not leftovers from a bygone era but recent initiatives launched by dedicated faculty and supportive administrators. I have hosted scores of such faculty and administrators at Columbia to observe classes, meet with faculty, and participate in workshops and seminars on liberal education. Among recent programs that have taken inspiration from Columbia's Core Curriculum are Ursinus College's Common Intellectual Experience, the University Core Curriculum at Seton Hall University, the Core Curriculum at Sacred Heart University, and the Columbia Common Core at Hostos Community College.[5] A full assortment of Core-oriented programs can be

---

5. For more information, see the websites for each of these programs: Common Intellectual Experience at Ursinus College, (https://www.ursinus.edu/academics

found under the umbrella of the Association for Core Texts and Course (ACTC), whose annual conference attracts hundreds of faculty and administrators from the US and abroad.

One noteworthy experiment in Core-text liberal education was launched at Purdue University's College of Liberal Arts in 2017. The Cornerstone Integrated Liberal Arts program is built around a two-semester sequence for first-year students in which they read, in chronological order, "Transformative Texts" from antiquity to the present. The program has revitalized the humanities at Purdue, attracting large numbers of STEM students as well as faculty from across the humanities and social sciences.[6] Students can go on to earn a certificate in liberal arts by following the first-year sequence, which fulfills part of the college's general education requirement, with thematically arranged courses that extend humanistic thinking into fields like engineering, technology, and the health sciences.

Inspired by the success of Cornerstone at Purdue, in late 2020 the National Endowment for the Humanities and the Teagle Foundation launched a multiyear initiative called Cornerstone: Learning for Living, which aims to "reinvigorate the role of the humanities in general education" through "shared experiences with transformative texts."[7] We have known for a long

---

/first-year-experience/common-intellectual-experience/), the Core Curriculum at Sacred Heart University (https://www.sacredheart.edu/academics/teaching- -learning/core-curriculum/curriculum-overview/), the University Core Curriculum at Seton Hall University (https://www.shu.edu/core-curriculum/index.cfm) and the Columbia Core at Hostos Community College (https://commons.hostos .cuny.edu/columbiacommoncoreathostos/).

6. See Melinda S. Zook, "Giant Leaps for the Liberal Arts at Purdue," in *Change: The Magazine of Higher Learning* 51:6 (Dec. 2019), pp. 45–51.

7. For more information on this initiative, visit http://www.teaglefoundation.org /Call-for-Proposals/Initiatives/Cornerstone.

time that there is an appetite among students for this kind of intellectually and personally transformative liberal education, especially when offered as a foundation to more career-oriented academic pathways. Much about the future of the humanities will depend on whether institutions remain committed to liberal education for all students and find innovative ways, like Purdue's Cornerstone Program, to keep it at the center of undergraduate education even as more and more students seek preprofessional and job-oriented degrees.

o o o

One of the dangers facing American higher education—and American civic culture in general—is a return to a time when liberal education was the exclusive province of a social elite. In the radical disruptions that have begun and will continue to reshape higher education, the most prestigious liberal arts colleges are likely to survive, if not unscathed, at least not fundamentally transformed. Many well-to-do families from the US and abroad will continue to seek—and pay for—a traditional liberal arts experience for their children. Moreover, alumni are not likely to turn their backs on their alma maters. But liberal education threatens to retreat to these bastions of privilege, with technical, vocational, and professional education, much of it online, for everyone else.

The animating argument of this book is for liberal education as the common education *for all*—not instead of a more practical education but as its prerequisite. Though I love liberal arts majors and was one myself, I am not advocating for more students to major in the liberal arts, but for liberal education to serve as the foundation for *every* major. I want nurses, computer scientists, accountants, engineers, entrepreneurs, lawyers, and professionals of every kind, to be liberally educated. We should not expect economically anxious families to forgo what seems to them the most stable or lucrative careers and instead study only the liberal arts. We—by which I mean college faculty and administrators—should eliminate the opportunity costs of liberal education by embedding it in every undergraduate degree. In turn, putting serious liberal arts programs at the center of the undergraduate curriculum will not only inspire more students to major in the liberal arts, but will reinvigorate the professoriate and reverse the precipitous decline in faculty jobs in the humanities.

The years ahead will be tumultuous for American colleges and universities. In the face of debilitating structural problems, public disinvestment, popular skepticism, and an unsustainable business model, the decade ahead will see a fundamental restructuring of higher education. The Covid-19 pandemic, still unfolding as this book went to press, will have a catastrophic impact on an "industry" already in crisis. Many institutions will not recover from the financial punishment the pandemic has inflicted; others will adapt in a way that makes them unrecognizable.

In this time of fundamental change, perhaps our greatest need is for clarity and conviction about the values and purposes of higher education. American colleges and universities have maintained the ideal of liberal learning through previous periods of upheaval. As with every crisis, our current ordeal also presents a set of opportunities. The corona virus pandemic has exposed the depth of social inequality in America and may give our generation the necessary spur to address it. Making liberal education available and accessible to all students is the most important contribution that higher education can make to this effort.

ACKNOWLEDGMENTS

To think about the people who have made this book possible is to think about the people who have made my life possible. It is beyond my power to adequately thank them all, and my attempts here necessarily fall short.

Mom gave me the most important thing, unreserved and unqualified love.

Dad taught me to love justice, to side with the underdog, and to believe that my ideas mattered.

My brother Keiselim Montás understands this book in a way that no one else can. He read each chapter, made corrections, suggested clarifications, and reminded me of things I had forgotten. He has been my companion through life. His support and encouragement have meant the world to me.

My brother Ray Acevedo read my early chapters and responded enthusiastically. His faith in my ability bring this project to completion buoyed me throughout the journey.

John Philippides read drafts of each chapter and offered appreciative and penetrating comments on nearly every paragraph. My debts to him—intellectual, psychological, filial—are greater than I can properly acknowledge. He has been more than a father to me.

From the day I walked into his undergraduate course on Foundations of American Literature, Andrew Delbanco has been my most important mentor and role model. Many years ago, when I first approached him about writing a dissertation on transcendentalism and abolitionism, he advised me—as his mentor Alan Heimert had advised him—to "tell it like a story." His intellectual generosity and interest in my development made all the difference in graduate school and in my career after that. As a writer, teacher, and thinker, his influence is evident throughout this book. After reading an early version of the manuscript, he also gave me key advice on structure and organization. Without his catalytic and—often enough—practical guidance, this book would never have come into being.

Paul Stern is the most lucid and incisive thinker about liberal education that I know. The year that he spent teaching in the Columbia Core Curriculum cemented a friendship that has been a great gift. My understanding of liberal education has been enriched and expanded by conversations with him in ways that no amount of individual research or cogitation could have produced. Paul read and responded to every page of this book; he was the first person to see any "completed" drafts. His constant support, steady wisdom, and depth of insight have made this a far better book than it would have been otherwise.

After my long tenure as Director of Columbia's Center for the Core Curriculum, Casey Blake performed institutional magic to bring me full-time to the Center for American Studies. His dedicated stewardship of the Freedom and Citizenship Program has changed the lives of many young people and enriched mine in innumerable ways. Along with Angela Darling and Laken King, he has made American Studies an oasis of sanity, collegiality, and good cheer.

My writing and revision process was sustained by generous friends, colleagues, and relatives who read and responded to various parts of the book. Damon Horowitz has been a key interlocutor and reader at every stage of this project. He understood and believed in what I was doing from the beginning. On the phone, on Zoom, walking in Fort Tryon Park or in the Redwood forests of Northern California, Damon's friendship and encouragement have been a ballast for me and the book.

Closer to home, Matthew Marco brought his incomparable eye for structure and design to the manuscript. One memorable summer evening, after our two-year-old boys had gone to bed, we sat on a bench outside the Mother Cabrini Shrine late into the night and talked with open hearts about Saint Augustine, faith, and fatherhood. His generosity, prescience, and steadfast friendship over this pandemic year have been invaluable gifts.

Robert Thomas, my collaborator in many renegade schemes, gave me encouragement and guided my explorations into the Columbia archives on the Core Curriculum. His friendship and his voracious mind were great aids in keeping me on task.

Paul and Sally Ross, my in-laws, but so much more, read my chapters as they were written and gave me feedback that made them more readable, to the point, and precise. Paul's writerly insights were especially valuable at moments when I wasn't sure I could get my message across to people who don't follow the inside-baseball of academia.

Richard Bozard, who long ago metamorphosed from former student to friend, chimed in from Richmond, Virginia, with oracular insights about the people I was writing about. I thank him for sharing his restless and wide-ranging mind with me.

At an early stage of this project, I had the opportunity to discuss it with Michael Olson during a visit to Saint Michael's College in Colchester, Vermont, and he subsequently read a draft of my chapter on Saint Augustine, giving me a bevy of helpful pointers.

Tim and Hannah Cassedy poured over my Freud chapter and gave me much needed perspective on how to talk about my experience of psychoanalysis. But far beyond that, their friend-ship, companionship, and love are among the great fortunes of my life.

Andreas Avgousti read my Augustine and Plato chapters and brought his considerable gifts as a teacher and political theorist to improving them.

Mara de Gennaro took a break from finalizing her own book manuscript to read and write with depth and sensitivity about my Augustine chapter. Her friendship and brilliance have been a rich source of pleasure and benefit ever since our time to-gether in graduate school.

Claudio Remeseira has been more than a friend and fellow-at-arms. He brought his exceptional editorial eye and intuition to help me think about the structure of the book and how to incorporate my story in a way that was digestible and accessible to a general reader.

Maura Spiegel, my co-pilot in the Introduction to American Studies course at Columbia, read a draft of my Freud chapter with frightening penetration and made suggestions that helped me recover it from what had become an unmanageable tangle.

The kind response of my neighbor Vicky Stein to my Augus-tine chapter was an early and much-needed vote of confidence.

David Denby, who has had his own powerful encounters with Great Books at Columbia, read my book proposal and gave me crucial encouragement and suggestions about the pos-sibilities of autobiographical writing.

Justine Blau assigned my Augustine chapter to her memoir-writing class at Lehman College and invited me to talk to the students. Their responses to the piece were among the most meaningful I received. I thank her and them for their generosity and openness.

The lifelong work of J. Scott Lee promoting Core texts and liberal education has contributed to my intellectual development in profound ways. He also offered generous encouragement and feedback throughout this project.

In 2008, when I took the position of Associate Dean of Academic Affairs and Director of the Center for the Core Curriculum at Columbia College, I inherited an administrative dream team: Janine de Novais, Elina Yuffa, and Clarence Coaxum. They taught me how to be an administrator and then enabled me to carry my vision of the Core far beyond Columbia. Later, the team would include Jamie Chandler, Toni Gunthrope-Hardee, Miosoty Checo, Karen Alvarez, Christine Butcher, Jessica Ng, David Truong, and Lidibeth Inoa. I thank them for all the ways in which they supported my work in the Core, for being absolutely dependable, and for always putting students ahead of administrative convenience.

In recent years, Roger Lehecka has been the kind of mentor and advisor to me for which he is famous among Columbia alumni. Although we never met while I was an undergraduate and he was Dean of Students, all the roads I traveled seemed in one way or another to point to him. I am used to encountering brilliance and even genius among my colleagues and students, but wisdom and virtue are much rarer. Roger embodies all of these qualities. His integrity and generosity have enriched my life in ways he probably cannot imagine.

One day Peter Dougherty took me to lunch at the Oyster Bar in Grand Central Station, and before our meal was over he had convinced me that I could write a book about liberal education. More than any other person, Peter is responsible for this book. His guidance, his encouragement, his incisive readings, and his ability to both reassure and challenge me, have made this book possible. He brought with him the incredible team at Princeton

University Press—among them Alena Chekanov, Brigitte Pelner, Bob Bettendorf, Patricia Fogarty, Karl Spurzem, Alyssa
Sanford, and Barbara Tonetti. They each contributed their considerable talent to making this book happen.

During the long pandemic winter of 2020–2021, the eight
parents and six (soon to be eight) children of the Hudson
Heights Alliance have stuck together with grace and valor.
When the grief of this season is no longer raw, the beauty of the
times we shared will stay with me.

Closest to home, closest to my heart, are Leigh and Arjuna.
Our lives are intertwined such that everything that I do belongs
to them and is due to them as much as to me.

INDEX

Jim Crow, 109
Joerling, Susan, 162–63
justice: Aristotle on, 60–61; Socrates on,
   78–81

Keppel, Frederic, 27–29
King, Martin Luther, Jr., 83, 98–99
Kronman, Anthony, 124

Laertius, Diogenes, 80
language acquisition, 52–54, 55
Latin American politics, 3–4, 26, 57–58
Lear, Jonathan, 131
Lelyveld, David, 188–89
"Letter from a Birmingham Jail," 98–99
liberal democracies, 47
liberal education, 1–2. *See also* Core
   Curriculum, Columbia College; as
   archaeological exercise, 54–55;
   Aristotle's definition of, 107–8;
   aura of frivolous self-indulgence
   surrounding, 12–13; brought to
   low-income students and families,
   10–12; as common education for all,
   224–25; content of, 109–10; as
   countercultural, 123–24; curricula
   design in, 73–74; delivering truth
   as basic task of, 84–85; diversity of
   voices in, 7; as education for freedom,
   107–10; Freedom and Citizenship
   program, 82–84; human freedom
   addressed by, 96; importance of,
   6–8; individual rights and, 108–9;
   inquiry into virtue in, 192–93;
   listening to conversation among
   greatest minds in, 193; for living
   meaningfully, 64–65; minority
   students steered away from, 34–35;
   modern understanding of, 2–3; in
   research universities, 124–31; role of

teacher in, 44; Scientific Revolution and, 204–5; search for genuine
   self-knowledge through, 110–12;
   Socrates as model for, 87–88; value-
   based judgment in, 190–92; viewed
   as waste of time, 6; Western classics
   role in, 211–12
Life of Antony, The, 46
Lincoln, Abraham, 83
Literature Humanities, Columbia, 18–20,
   21–23, 29, 35, 55–56, 67; course
   objectives, 23–24, 26; modeled on
   Erskine's General Honors course,
   23–25
Locke, John, 83

Macbeth, 85
Madison, James, 60
Marxism, 3–4, 26, 122, 206
Mehta, P. J., 170
Meno, 54
metaphysics, 99, 102–6, 183–85
Mill, John Stuart, 90
Milton, John, 7
mindfulness, 117
minority students, 33–35
Montaigne, Michele de, 84
Montás, Roosevelt: on Aristotle's
   treatment of poetry, 67–68; arrival at
   Columbia College, 1, 29–32; arrival
   in the United States, 5, 38–39;
   becomes an American citizen,
   176–77; childhood of, 3–4, 5, 38–40,
   49–51; described by Wallace Gray
   as "cocky," 68–69; as Director of
   Center for the Core Curriculum,
   210–11; dreams of, 154–58; early
   experience in teaching, 142–44;
   experience with psychoanalysis,
   134–40, 160–61; father of, 3–4,